READING PALETTE

Blue

Katsuhiko Muto   Bill Benfield

photographs by
iStockphoto
PIXTA

音声ファイルのダウンロード／ストリーミング

CD マーク表示がある箇所は、音声を弊社 HP より無料でダウンロード／ストリーミングすることができます。下記 URL の書籍詳細ページに音声ダウンロードアイコンがございますのでそちらから自習用音声としてご活用ください。

https://seibido.co.jp/ad710

Reading Palette Blue —Intermediate—

Copyright © 2025 by Katsuhiko Muto, Bill Benfield

All rights reserved for Japan.
No part of this book may be reproduced in any form
without permission from Seibido Co., Ltd.

はしがき

　Reading Palette は、習熟度（初級〜中級）に適した語数からなる英文パッセージを理解することを通して、英語リーディングに必要な文法やスキルを身につけることを主眼とした教科書シリーズです。

　SNS のメッセージに目を通す時、ネットニュースをチェックする時、課題のために集めた資料を熟読する時、文学作品を吟味する時などを思い浮かべると、同じ「読む」でもずいぶん違う活動であることが分かるのではないでしょうか。日本語で書かれたものであればこのような切り替えは自然にできるのですが、「英語リーディング」となると、語彙や文法の理解にとらわれてしまい、対象や目的に応じた読み方ができなくなってしまいます。

　限られた時間の中で英文を手際良く読解するスキルが求められる現代では、リーディングに特化した英文法（リーディング・グラマー）を学習し、英文に応じた多面的な読み方（リーディング・スキル）を身につけることは必須です。絵を描く際、青はパレットに最初に出される基本色のひとつですが、同様に本書（Blue）のテーマ（クリティカル・リーディング）はリーディング・パレットに必須な「色」です。本書では英語で与えられる情報、そこに含まれる著者の意見を能動的に分析、理解することを通して、批判的な英文の読み方を体得します。

　本書の英文パッセージは、世界中から集めたニュースや出来事、事実や新しい発見に関する話題を中心に扱っています。社会生活に密接に関係する身近な話題に触れ、学生たちが「面白い！」、「なるほど」と感銘を受けることで内容理解が進み、同時に語彙や文法、リーディングスキルをより自然な形で身に付けられるよう工夫しています。本書を用いた授業を通して、新しい知識とともに実践的な英語リーディング力を有する学生が一人でも増えてくれることを著者一同、心から願っております。

　最後になりましたが、著者の思いを共有して最後までご尽力頂いた成美堂の中澤ひろ子様に心からお礼を申し上げます。

2024年夏
武藤克彦
Bill Benfield

本書の使い方

　各章は Reading Passage（英文パッセージ）に先行する Before You Read（前提知識の活性化）、パッセージに続く Test Yourself（理解度の確認）、Follow-up（発展的学習）、Wrap-up（学習のまとめ）の構成になっています。

Before You Read

　英文リーディングのためのウォームアップです。章のタイトルとその説明文に目を通した後、5つの英文をもとに、各自トピックに関する背景知識の有無を確認します。

Reading Passage

　各章の中心となる英文パッセージです。事前に予習する場合でも最初は辞書などを使用せず、右側の Vocabulary（語注）を頼りに最後まで読み通します。

Test Yourself

A Overview

　英文のペアから、パッセージの内容と合致している文を選択する問題です。文構造や選択肢の語句が似ている場合があるので精読が求められる問題です。

B Focus on Details

　パッセージで与えられた詳細情報について問う問題です。語彙だけでなく、文法に関する問題も含まれます。質問文を精読してから、4つの選択肢を判別します。

iv

Follow-up

A Zoom In

　クリティカル・リーディングに関する知識を深めるセクションです。パッセージと照らし合わせながら学習して、批判的な読解方法を身につけます。

B Discussion

　ペアまたはグループで行うディスカッションです。2つのトピックのうち、前者は比較的容易なトピック、後者は発展的なトピックになっています。

Wrap-up

A Build Your Vocabulary

　英語で与えられる語義をもとに、パッセージから該当する単語を探して記入する問題です。語義に合うようにパッセージ内の語を原形に直して記入します。例）advances → advance

B Summary & Dictation

　空所に適する語彙を考えながら、パッセージの要約を考える問題です。解答を記入した後、音声で解答を確認します。

CONTENTS

Chapter 1 p.09
Human Intelligence
Reading Passages — Are We Getting Dumber?
Reading Skill — クリティカル・リーディングとは

Chapter 2 p.15
Social Media
Reading Passages — The Clock Is "Tik-ing" for Facebook
Reading Skill — プレ・リーディングとは

Chapter 3 p.21
Working Dogs
Reading Passages — Lending a Helping Paw
Reading Skill — プレ・リーディング1：目的を考える

Chapter 4 p.27
15-minute City
Reading Passages — Everything on Your Doorstep
Reading Skill — プレ・リーディング2：周辺情報を活用する

Chapter 5 p.33
Tiny Houses
Reading Passages — Moving to Minimalism
Reading Skill — プレ・リーディング3：関連語彙をスキャニングする

Chapter 6 p.39
Powering Our Homes
Reading Passages — Saying Goodbye to Gas
Reading Skill — プレ・リーディング4：パラグラフ冒頭をスキミングする

Chapter 7 p.45
The Future of Cars
Reading Passages — Cars — Who Needs Them?
Reading Skill — ホワイル・リーディングとは

Chapter 8 — p.51
Superhumans
- **Reading Passages**: Leaving Our Old Selves Behind
- **Reading Skill**: ホワイル・リーディング1：自問自答しながら読む

Chapter 9 — p.57
Restaurants in Crisis
- **Reading Passages**: Kitchen Staff — Workers or Slaves?
- **Reading Skill**: ホワイル・リーディング2：事実と意見を区別する

Chapter 10 — p.63
Lab-grown Meat
- **Reading Passages**: Better Than the Real Thing?
- **Reading Skill**: ホワイル・リーディング3：推測・予測する

Chapter 11 — p.69
Van Living
- **Reading Passages**: Time to Hit the Road
- **Reading Skill**: ホワイル・リーディング4：注釈をつける

Chapter 12 — p.75
Sportswashing
- **Reading Passages**: Let Sports Clean Up Your Image
- **Reading Skill**: ポスト・リーディングとは

Chapter 13 — p.81
Board Games and Climate Change
- **Reading Passages**: Everyone Is a Winner
- **Reading Skill**: ポスト・リーディング1：情報を抽出する

Chapter 14 — p.87
The Gig Economy
- **Reading Passages**: Freedom or Security?
- **Reading Skill**: ポスト・リーディング2：概要をまとめる

Chapter 15 — p.93
Digital Music
- **Reading Passages**: Are Computers Destroying Music?
- **Reading Skill**: ポスト・リーディング3：反応する

Chapter 1 Human Intelligence

近年の高度な科学技術の進歩を見るにつけ、人類はより賢くなっていると考えてしまいますが、実はこの30年間人間のIQスコアは低下し続けているのです。なぜなのでしょうか。そもそもIQとは何を表す数値なのでしょうか。

 Before You Read

Complete the sentences below.

1. Research has shown that average IQ scores have been [declining / increasing] since the 1980s.
2. In modern-day society, more and more work relies on [physical strength / abstract thinking].
3. Chemical pollutants have been shown to interfere with our [hormonal / intellectual] balance.
4. The constant flow of information from our digital devices has [sharpened / shortened] our attention span.
5. Certain types of intelligence [deteriorate / improve] with advanced age.

Are We Getting Dumber?

1 When I think about the **astounding** scientific and technological advances that the human race has achieved in recent years, I would like to think that as a species, we are becoming smarter and smarter. But unfortunately, it seems that the evidence is currently pointing in the opposite direction, at least **as far as** IQ scores **are concerned**. A rather depressing Norwegian study in 2004 showed that, after decades of increase, average IQ scores have been in steady decline since the 1990s, and experts are struggling to understand why.

2 Up to that point, the story had been very different. In the 1980s, American researcher James Flynn analyzed the results of millions of IQ tests conducted over decades in many different countries and discovered something remarkable: they showed that people were getting smarter. Starting in 1930, average scores were increasing by four points every decade. Several theories attempted to **account for** this phenomenon (**dubbed** "the Flynn effect"), including better medical care, improved nutrition, and a higher standard of education, at least in developed countries. Another was a widespread transition from manual labor to work that required a high degree of abstract thinking, which is what IQ tests are designed to measure.

3 How then do we account for the current drop? Some **ascribe** it to environmental factors. Since the 1970s, it is estimated that the amount of chemical **pollutants** around us has increased 300-**fold**. Several of these have been shown to interfere with our hormonal balance, especially regarding the normal functioning of the **thyroid gland**, which is crucial in brain development.

4 Personally, I strongly suspect that the most crucial factor is the cognitive challenges we face in a data-**saturated** society, where the constant **bombardment** of information from digital devices makes us more and more distracted and shortens our attention span. Also, I believe that the wealth of information available at the touch of a button, as with smartphone navigation, means that we no longer need to develop our mental faculties **to the same extent** we did in a pre-digital era. Alternatively, it could simply be that with the **profusion of** information coming at us from all directions, we may have lost the capacity to distinguish what is important and meaningful from what is trivial and unnecessary. Yet another **body of** research suggests that our aging society is responsible. People are now living longer, and certain types of intelligence decline with advanced age.

5 Despite this rather gloomy **outlook**, I think it would be wrong to be discouraged. I am convinced that IQ is actually a rather narrow measure of human ability, and one that prioritizes **abstract reasoning** over other areas such as **empathy** and physical or artistic skills, which are perhaps even more important in helping us to lead a happy, fulfilled, and creative life.

 **Test Yourself**

A Overview

Read the passage and choose the correct statement from each pair.

1. a) There is no doubt that human beings as a species are getting smarter.
   b) The trend of increasing IQ scores has now gone into reverse.

2. a) Intelligence tests were originally developed to determine which children needed help with learning.
   b) Intelligence tests were originally developed to identify the most intelligent children.

3. a) James Flynn published his research into IQ in the 1930s.
   b) The "Flynn effect" became widely known in the 1980s.

4. a) Cognitive factors are recognized as the only factor in declining IQ scores.
   b) Environmental factors are just one explanation of the decline in IQ scores.

5. a) IQ is generally accepted to be the most reliable indicator of overall intelligence.
   b) IQ scores do not represent the entire range of people's abilities.

B Focus on Details

Read the passage again and complete each sentence.

1. Progress in science and technology may show that human beings as a _____ are getting smarter.
   a) spectacle   b) specialization   c) species   d) specific

2. The _____ that we are becoming more intelligent has now started pointing in the opposite direction.
   a) transition   b) evidence   c) research   d) origin

3. Several theories have been put forward to _____ for the decline in average IQ scores.
   a) account   b) explain   c) describe   d) analyze

4. Chemical pollutants can _____ with the normal functioning of hormones in our body.
   a) bother   b) disturb   c) destroy   d) interfere

5. IQ scores are not the only measure of our abilities, so the results should not make us feel _____.
   a) discounted   b) discouraged   c) disgusted   d) disapproved

Chapter 1　Human Intelligence

A　Zoom In

クリティカル・リーディングとは

自動翻訳が容易な時代に英文読解で求められるのは、英文を通して与えられた情報や著者の意見を**批判的・批評的に（critically）読み解く**こと、それに対して能動的、主体的に反応することです。この章の英文であれば、以下のように著者の意見（提案）が明確に述べられている箇所では一歩立ち止まって「本当だろうか」と疑ってみましょう。

- Personally, I strongly suspect that . . .（個人的に〜ではと私は強く疑う）
- Also, I believe . . .（私は〜と確信する）
- I think it would be wrong to . . .（私は〜と考える）

クリティカル・リーディング（critical reading）には①**プレ・リーディング**（読む前の事前準備）、②**ホワイル・リーディング**（読解と同時に行う作業）、③**ポスト・リーディング**（読後の振り返り）の３つの段階があります。英文読解の最中だけでなく、読み始める前や読み終えた後にも行うべき活動があります。

B　Discussion

Discuss the following statements or questions.

1. Have you ever felt overwhelmed by a flood of information given by digital devices? How did you deal with it?

2. Research EQ (Emotional Quotient) and AQ (Adversity Quotient). Discuss how they are important for us to survive in a highly digital world.

13

Chapter 1   Human Intelligence

Wrap-up

A Build Your Vocabulary

Find the words in the reading passage that match the definitions below.

1. (line 15) unusual or interesting   = _____
2. (line 21) a change from one form or type to another   = _____
3. (line 22) existing as an idea, not as a material object   = _____
4. (line 28) to try to stop something from happening   = _____
5. (line 31) extremely important   = _____
6. (line 38) an inherent capability, power, or function   = _____
7. (line 42) having little value or importance   = _____
8. (line 50) to treat something as more important than other things = _____

B Summary & Dictation

07

Listen and complete the sentences using these words.

- decline
- transition
- cognitive
- distracted
- pollutants
- factors
- profusion
- gloomy
- nutrition
- prioritizes

A U.S. researcher discovered that IQ scores rose steadily from 1930 onward. Various theories were put forward to explain this including improved medical care, better ①[   ], and a large-scale ②[   ] in society toward jobs that required abstract thinking. But then, in 2004, a study showed that there has been an ongoing ③[   ] in IQ scores since the 1990s. Environmental ④[   ] such as a growth in chemical ⑤[   ] is one possible explanation. Another is the fact that we now face ⑥[   ] challenges as the ⑦[   ] of information from our digital devices makes us more ⑧[   ]. This outlook may seem rather ⑨[   ], but we must bear in mind that IQ is only a narrow measure of intelligence that ⑩[   ] abstract reasoning over other important areas such as empathy or artistic and physical skills.

14

Chapter 2

Social Media

世界で最も利用者の多い **SNS** は依然として **Facebook** ですが、近年は新規参入者の数が低迷しています。それに対して **TikTok** ユーザーの数は過去10年間で若者を中心に爆発的に増えています。2つの **SNS** の違いはどこにあるのでしょう。

Before You Read

Complete the sentences below.

1. On a global scale, the biggest social media platform is [Facebook / Line].

2. Facebook is acquiring new users at a [faster / slower] pace than it used to.

3. By 2022, TikTok had [almost reached / acquired] one billion users.

4. TikTok provides its users with a [wider / narrower] range of interactive content than Facebook does.

5. Facebook has introduced some new features that [seem to copy / are very different from] those offered by TikTok.

The Clock Is "Tik-ing" for Facebook

1   Among social media platforms, Facebook is still far ahead of any of its competitors, with an estimated 2 billion global users in the fourth **quarter** of 2022. Despite this, Facebook's management believes the company is facing a problem. While the number of users is still growing, since the mid 2010s the rate of increase has slowed considerably compared to the **phenomenal** pace at which the company added new users in the past.

2   There are several reasons behind this **slowdown**. An obvious one is that Facebook has already acquired most Internet users in developed countries, and so there is little room left for expansion in those markets. Facebook has also **come in for** sharp criticism regarding privacy and data security. The research firm Cambridge Analytica was able to obtain personal data for millions of Facebook users without their consent and then use this information to try to influence the 2016 US presidential campaign. Moreover, users complain that their **newsfeed** contains more and more ads rather than posts from friends, leading some of them to reduce their engagement with the platform or abandon it entirely.

3   One major cause of concern for Facebook, however, is **demographic** change. Put quite simply, Facebook's user base is getting older, while younger people prefer newer rivals whose features and mode of presentation **align** more closely **with** their interests. Facebook's main rival is TikTok. Between 2014 and 2022, this China-based social media platform acquired one billion users, almost all of whom are young.

Vocabulary

quarter 四半期

phenomenal 驚異的な

slowdown 低迷

come in for ~
（批判など）を受ける

newsfeed 配信ニュース

demographic
（利用者）層

align with ~
～と肩を並べる

4　TikTok users will be well aware of the host of attractive features it offers. Unlike Facebook, it gives users the space to showcase their own singing, dancing, or **lip-synching** talents through the medium of short videos, with the added plus of using effects and filters to **personalize** content and make it more entertaining. By focusing mainly on user-generated content, TikTok also creates a strong sense of community, giving users the opportunity to interact and even collaborate with others on the platform. TikTok's **algorithm** also differs from Facebook's **in that** it aims to supply users with a wide range of content, enabling them to continually make new discoveries and explore different genres.

5　Facebook has attempted to deal with its competitors in two main ways: by either purchasing them or copying them. When Instagram and WhatsApp emerged as threats, Facebook simply acquired the companies. **Faced with** the enormous popularity of TikTok's user-generated short videos, Facebook introduced Reels, which was an attempt at creating its own similar feature. **Given that** social media apps barely existed 20 years ago, it is intriguing to **speculate** what the coming 20 years might bring, and whether Facebook will be able to survive demographic change, increasing **disillusionment** with its offerings, and the presence of newer, **snappier** rivals.

---

lip-synch ロパクで歌う

personalize 個人向けに変更するかカスタマイズする

algorithm アルゴリズム（一連の計算方法）
in that ~ ~という点において

faced with ~ ~に直面して

given that ~ ~を考慮すると
speculate ~ ~を推測する

disillusionment 失望

snappy 勢いのある

A Overview

Read the passage and choose the correct statement from each pair.

1. a) As of 2023, Facebook was still the world's largest social media platform by a wide margin.
   b) Some of Facebook's newer and younger rivals are about to surpass it in popularity.

2. a) Facebook has been criticized for not keeping user data and privacy secure.
   b) Facebook has been praised for providing its services in developing countries.

3. a) Facebook is now mainly trying to acquire more users from older generations.
   b) Facebook is concerned that it is not attracting as many younger users as it once did.

4. a) Interaction and collaboration among users is one of TikTok's major points of appeal.
   b) Unlike TikTok, Facebook enables users to make new discoveries and explore different genres.

5. a) Despite competition, Facebook's policy is always to offer completely new services to attract new users.
   b) When faced with competition from rival companies, Facebook usually either purchases them or copies them.

B Focus on Details

Read the passage again and complete each sentence.

1. With an estimated 2 billion global users, Facebook is _____ ahead of any of its competitors.
   a) long   b) much   c) far   d) most

2. _____ its user numbers are still growing, Facebook's rate of increase has slowed considerably since the mid 2010s.
   a) With   b) When   c) Since   d) While

3. Facebook has already acquired most Internet users in developed countries, and so there is _____ room left for expansion in those markets.
   a) little   b) a little   c) few   d) a few

4. Between 2014 and 2022, TikTok managed to acquire one billion users, almost all of _____ are young.
   a) who   b) whom   c) these   d) those

5. _____ that social media apps barely existed 20 years ago, it is intriguing to speculate what the coming 20 years might bring.
   a) Because   b) Despite   c) Assuming   d) Given

Chapter 2　Social Media

A　Zoom In

プレ・リーディング とは

英文に目を通す前に「**事前準備する**」ことからクリティカル・リーディングは始まります。この準備段階を**プレ・リーディング**（pre-reading）と言いますが、この段階では次のような作業を行います。

1. 目的を考える
   目の前の英文を読む目的を自分自身で考える
2. 周辺情報を活用する
   英文以外から得られる情報に着目しそれを活用する
3. スキミング（概略読み）する
   英文タイトルをヒントに文中から関連語句を探す
4. スキミング（概略読み）する
   英文全体にざっと目を通して英文の構成を確認する

本章の英文タイトル the clock is "Tik-ing" for Facebook についても「Tik-ing とはどんな意味だろう」「どのような情報が述べられるだろう」のように思考を巡らすことにより脳が活性化します。このような事前準備により読解スピードだけでなく結果的な理解度も深まるのです。

B　Discussion

Discuss the following statements or questions.

1. Do you use any social media platform? Discuss good and bad points about it.

2. Based on the information provided in the reading passage, compare Facebook with TikTok in terms of advantages and disadvantages.

Chapter 2　Social Media

A Build Your Vocabulary

Find the words in the reading passage that match the definitions below.

1. (line 2) a rival that can offer a similar service　=　_____

2. (line 12) the process of becoming greater in size　=　_____

3. (line 16) permission or agreement to do something　=　_____

4. (line 20) being involved with something at a particular time　=　_____

5. (line 20) to give up doing something completely　=　_____

6. (line 32) to exhibit or display　=　_____

7. (line 41) to examine something to learn more about it　=　_____

8. (line 50) extremely interesting　=　_____

B Summary & Dictation

 13

Complete the paragraph with the words below. Change the word form if necessary. Listen to the passage to check the answers.

•acquire　•shun　•demographic　•discover　•aware
•person　•collaborate　•opportunity　•supply　•showcase

One major concern for Facebook is ①[　　　　　] change. Facebook's user base is getting older, while younger people are ②[　　　　　] it in favor of newer rivals. Facebook's main competitor is TikTok. Between 2014 and 2022, this China-based social media platform managed to ③[　　　　　] one billion users, almost all of whom are young. Those who already use TikTok will be well ④[　　　　　] of its attractive features. Unlike Facebook, it gives users the space to ⑤[　　　　　] their own singing, dancing, or lip-synching talents through short videos, with the added plus of using effects and filters to ⑥[　　　　　] content and make it more entertaining. By focusing on user-generated content, TikTok also creates a sense of community among its viewers, giving them the ⑦[　　　　　] to interact and even ⑧[　　　　　] with others. TikTok's algorithm also differs from Facebook's by ⑨[　　　　　] users with a wide range of content, enabling them to continually make new ⑩[　　　　　] and explore different genres.

Chapter 3

Working Dogs

犬は心身によい影響を与えてくれます。その効果を必要とする動物介在療法のような専門的分野においては適性検査と長期訓練が必要となるため、ひっ迫する需要に応えることができていません。解決策はあるのでしょうか。

Before You Read

Complete the sentences below.

1. Dogs have unique abilities that can help human beings in a [wide / narrow] range of activities.
2. Facility dog handlers are [volunteers / trained professionals].
3. Facility dogs are [allowed to work in / prohibited from entering] a hospital's intensive care unit.
4. The number of trained working dogs [exceeds / cannot meet] the demand for them.
5. "Service dog" [is another name for / differs from] "facility dog."

Reading Passage

Lending a Helping Paw

1   The old saying that dogs are "man's best friend" may well be true, but it only tells part of the story. While dogs provide loyalty and companionship, they also have unique skills that can be **harnessed** to help human beings in a wide range of tasks, from herding animals on farms to sniffing out **contraband** at ports.

2   One important area in which dogs play a major role is what is known as animal-assisted therapy. Research has **established** that animals can have a strong effect on people's physical and psychological well-being while also improving mood and quality of life. Dogs are ideally suited to this kind of role because, with the right training, they are obedient and **empathetic**. Consequently, they can often be **deployed** to provide support in institutions such as hospitals, nursing homes, and even prisons. Dogs that are **assigned** to work full-time in this way are known as facility dogs.

3   There is one such program in Japan. It is run by the non-profit organization (NPO) Shine On! Kids and is **designed** to give emotional support and encouragement to children who are hospitalized for long periods with cancer and other serious illnesses. The dogs are extremely well trained, and their handlers are **qualified** and experienced nurses, and so they are even allowed to perform their work inside the intensive care unit.

4   Selection and training, however, create an obstacle to the development of such programs. Dogs must be sourced from specialist breeders, who can pick animals with the right

temperament even when they are very young. These dogs then have to undergo a years-long and costly training
30 program before they can be assigned. It should **come as no surprise**, then, to learn that the demand for these dogs far **outstrips** the number available.

5　One organization that is trying to **address** this problem is Atlas Assistance Dogs. It focuses on so-called
35 service dogs, which differ from **facility dogs** in that they are assigned to one particular individual. This is usually someone with a disability who wants to lead a more active and independent life. Atlas's core belief is that anyone who needs a service dog should be able to have one, but it is
40 often difficult to get one from an organization because the waiting list is so long. Atlas has therefore developed a program that allows people with disabilities to train and **certify** their own dogs with the help of its skilled volunteer trainers.

45 **6**　One important consideration is that, whether the training is handled **exclusively** by specialists or by individual owners assisted by specialists, we must ensure that the welfare of the dogs is highly valued. If the dogs are going to spend their lives helping human beings, we
50 have an obligation to respect them **in return**.

---

temperament
気性、気質

come as no surprise
驚くには当たらない

outstrip ~ ～を上回る

address ～に取り組む

facility dog
施設に常駐する犬、ファ
シリティドッグ

certify ~ ～を認定する

exclusively
もっぱら、独占的に

in return お返しに

 Test Yourself

A Overview

Read the passage and choose the correct statement from each pair.

1. a) Dogs are naturally inclined and able to help human beings.
   b) Working dogs need to be trained to use their unique skills.

2. a) Dogs can positively affect people both physically and psychologically.
   b) Training a dog can help improve people's mood and quality of life.

3. a) Shine On! Kids is a specialist dog breeding and training organization.
   b) The mission of Shine On! Kids is to support children with serious illnesses.

4. a) Atlas Assistance Dogs supplies well-trained dogs to a variety of organizations.
   b) Atlas Assistance Dogs allows disabled people to help train their own dogs.

5. a) Atlas Assistance Dogs tries to help disabled people become more self-reliant.
   b) Atlas Assistance Dogs is an organization run by disabled people to help others like them.

B Focus on Details

Read the passage again and complete each sentence.

1. Dogs play a large role in animal-_____ therapy.
   a) assisting   b) assisted   c) assist   d) assistant

2. Dogs are ideally _____ providing therapeutic care because they are obedient and empathetic.
   a) trained in   b) convenient for   c) responsible for   d) suited to

3. The demand for dogs far _____ the number available.
   a) outstrips   b) outruns   c) outsources   d) outdoes

4. Selection and training create an obstacle _____ the development of such programs.
   a) against   b) from   c) to   d) beside

5. Dogs can have a strong _____ on people's physical and psychological well-being.
   a) effect   b) result   c) reaction   d) affect

Chapter 3　Working Dogs

プレ・リーディング1：目的を考える

プレ・リーディングの最初のステップは英文を読む「**目的を考える**」ことです。授業課題の場合でも、一瞬立ち止まって自分自身に以下の質問をしてみましょう。それによって自分なりの目的を持って読解に立ち向かうことができます。

- この英文を読む「自分自身の」目的は何か。
- トピックに興味があるか・ないか。なぜそうなのか。
- 英文からどのような情報や知識を得られそうか、期待したいか。
- どのような英語学習の効果（〜に関する語彙など）が得られるか。

この英文の場合はどうでしょうか。Lending a Helping Paw というタイトルから何が思い浮かぶでしょうか。トピックに対する興味はどのくらいでしょうか。どのような語彙が登場すると思いますか。同じ授業、同じ英文であっても個々人の目的意識は異なります。読む目的を考えることは受動的な読み方から脱却するための第一歩です。

B Discussion

Discuss the following statements or questions.

1. Do you feel soothed when a puppy is around you? Whether yes or no, why is that?

2. Discuss what makes service dogs stressed out and how people should keep company with them.

Chapter 3 Working Dogs

A Build Your Vocabulary

Find the words in the reading passage that match the definitions below.

1. (line 3) enjoyment of spending time with other people = _____
2. (line 12) willing to do what someone tells you to do = _____
3. (line 19) action of giving someone support or confidence = _____
4. (line 21) to a very great degree = _____
5. (line 25) difficulty preventing you achieving something = _____
6. (line 29) to experience something unpleasant or difficult = _____
7. (line 38) not relying on someone else = _____
8. (line 50) something you must do = _____

B Summary & Dictation

Complete the paragraph with the words below. Change the word form if necessary. Listen to the passage to check the answers.

| •undergo | •institution | •companionship | •disability | •certify |
| •provide | •harness | •select | •obedient | •psychological |

Dogs provide us with loyalty and ①[   ], but they also have unique skills that can be ②[   ] to help us in a variety of ways. One is in animal-assisted therapy. Animals can have a strong effect on people's physical and ③[   ] well-being. Dogs are ideally suited to this kind of role because they are ④[   ] and empathetic, and so they can often provide support in ⑤[   ]. The NPO Shine On! Kids ⑥[   ] facility dogs to support children hospitalized for long periods with serious illnesses. ⑦[   ] and training, however, are an obstacle. Dogs have to ⑧[   ] a long and costly training program before they can be assigned, and so the demand outstrips the number available. Atlas Assistance Dogs believes that anyone who needs a service dog should be able to have one, and so has developed a program that allows people with ⑨[   ] to train and ⑩[   ] their own dogs with the help of its skilled volunteer trainers.

Chapter 4

15-minute City

レジャー施設や病院など日常生活に必要な施設が自宅から徒歩や自転車で15分圏内にある「15分都市」。パリ市長アンヌ・イダルゴにより推進された都市計画構想ですが、実現可能な都市にはどのような特徴があるのでしょう。

Before You Read

Complete the sentences below.

1. The historical centers of older European cities are often full of [narrow / broad] streets.
2. Throughout the 20th century, city planners mostly prioritized the needs of [automobiles / pedestrians].
3. The Mayor of Paris recently [praised / criticized] the idea of the 15-minute city.
4. The COVID-19 pandemic brought about a [limited / widespread] shift to working from home.
5. A [minority / majority] of the world's population lives in cities.

27

Everything on Your Doorstep

1   Whenever I visit the historical centers of European cities such as Florence, their narrow, winding streets **crammed** full of shops, restaurants, and workshops never fail to delight me. They make me long for the time when cities were designed for people rather than automobiles. But sadly, the unstoppable rise of car culture throughout the 20th century led city planners to prioritize the needs of drivers over pedestrians. Building the necessary infrastructure for automobiles, such as roads, tunnels, and parking lots, **gobbled up** precious urban space, pushing residents and shops into **far-flung** suburbs. It has also led to health hazards such as air and noise pollution, and the risk of traffic accidents.

2   However, there are reasons for optimism. The quest to make our cities more livable and people-focused has led to a number of proposed solutions. One is the idea of "the 15-minute city." The idea was **thrust into** the mainstream by Anne Hidalgo, who has served as Mayor of Paris since 2014. As part of her 2020 election campaign, she pledged to create 15-minute cities in the French capital. She was inspired by Carlos Moreno, a professor at Paris's Sorbonne university, who **coined** the phrase in 2016. He believes that as we emerge from an oil-based economy and move into a "post-vehicle era," we need to reinvent the idea of what he calls "urban proximity." His vision is that city residents should have access to virtually all they need, including shops, leisure facilities, and even medical care, within a 15-minute walk or bicycle ride of their home.

3 **Measures** to combat the COVID-19 pandemic boosted the idea. Not only were people's movements severely restricted, there was also a widespread shift to working from home. Many people therefore became accustomed to spending more time in their own neighborhood, and so the idea of a more local lifestyle with easy access to necessary amenities began to seem appealing.

4 But the 15-minute city also has its critics. Some say that while it is suited to Europe, where cities are mostly designed on a traditional model, it would be much harder to **implement** in the US, where most people live in **sprawling** suburbs and are forced to rely on cars. There is also a socioeconomic aspect to consider. While the 15-minute city may be **feasible** in affluent urban districts that are already well-stocked with shops and other amenities, it is less easy to imagine the concept succeeding in poorer neighborhoods with fewer jobs, shops, and amenities.

5 Despite the criticism, I firmly believe that the 15-minute city is a solution to our most pressing urban problems. **All in all**, it is an invaluable contribution to the debate on how to improve life in cities, which are already home to most of the world's population.

---

measures（複）方策

implement ~
~を実践する
sprawling
不規則に拡大した

feasible 実現可能な

all in all 全体的に見て

A Overview

Read the passage and choose the correct statement from each pair.

1. a) In the past, European cities were people-focused rather than automobile-focused.
   b) Narrow, winding streets can be found everywhere in European cities.

2. a) The rise of car culture increased the population of city centers.
   b) The rise of car culture forced people and shops to relocate from city centers to suburbs.

3. a) Carlos Moreno was elected as Mayor of Paris thanks to his idea of the 15-minute city.
   b) The 15-minute city was a central idea in Anne Hidalgo's re-election campaign in 2020.

4. a) The 15-minute city is seen as a promising way to revitalize poorer neighborhoods.
   b) Richer districts are more suitable for implementation of the 15-minute city idea.

5. a) Cities in the US and in Europe are broadly similar in the way they are laid out.
   b) In many US cities, people live in suburbs and rely on cars in daily life.

B Focus on Details

Read the passage again and complete each sentence.

1. The number of automobiles continued to increase _____ the 20th century.
   a) prior to   b) throughout   c) following   d) along

2. Exhaust emissions from millions of cars has led to environmental _____.
   a) degradation   b) degraded   c) degrade   d) degrading

3. During the COVID-19 pandemic, people's movements were _____ in many countries.
   a) restrained   b) respected   c) rescheduled   d) restricted

4. During the pandemic, people became more accustomed _____ spending more time at home.
   a) to   b) for   c) with   d) on

5. In poorer neighborhoods, jobs, shops, and amenities are in short _____.
   a) provision   b) availability   c) supply   d) range

Chapter 4 15-minute City

Follow-up

A Zoom In

プレ・リーディング2：周辺情報を活用する

プレ・リーディングで確認するのはタイトルだけではありません。英文に付随する写真やイラスト、グラフや図表、質問といった「**周辺情報を活用する**」ことが背景知識の活性化につながります。情報の有無を確認して、それ元に以下を自問自答しましょう。

- ・視覚情報（写真やイラスト）から何が想像できるか。
- ・データ（図表やグラフ）はどのような情報を示しているか。
- ・見出しやリード（短い要約）、説明文から何が理解できるか。
- ・これらの情報は英文とどのように関係しているのか。

本書では英文に先行する写真やイラスト、その説明文や Before You Read の質問が重要な情報源になります。真剣に考えて解答することで、トピックと自分自身の経験・知識が関連付けられ、批判的読解の準備が整います。

B Discussion

Discuss the following statements or questions.

1. Is it feasible to transform your hometown into a 15-minute city? How? Why not?

2. Besides the idea of the 15-minute city, discuss ideas how we can make our towns more livable and people-focused.

Chapter 4   15-minute City

Wrap-up

A Build Your Vocabulary

Find the words in the reading passage that match the definitions below.

1. (line 7) to decide which is the most important to deal with it first = _____
2. (line 19) to promise seriously and formally = _____
3. (line 20) to make someone want to do something = _____
4. (line 22) to come forth, appear = _____
5. (line 25) closeness or nearness in place or time etc. = _____
6. (line 35) something that provides comfort or pleasure = _____
7. (line 43) having a large amount of money or owning a lot of things = _____
8. (line 48) needing immediate attention = _____

B Summary & Dictation

 26

Complete the paragraph with the words below. Change the word form if necessary. Listen to the passage to check the answers.

| • unstoppable | • critics | • in mind | • accustom | • sprawl |
| • concept | • within | • prioritize | • appeal | • point out |

In the past, cities were designed with people ①[   ], but nowadays, city planners tend to ②[   ] the needs of drivers over those of pedestrians. The ③[   ] rise of car culture has led to limited urban space being claimed for automobile infrastructure, forcing people and shops to move to far-flung suburbs. The 15-minute city ④[   ], popularized by the Mayor of Paris, aims to redesign cities so that residents have all they need for a comfortable life ⑤[   ] a 15-minute walk or bicycle ride from their homes. The idea became more ⑥[   ] during the COVID-19 pandemic, when many people became ⑦[   ] to working from home and spending more time in their own neighborhood. ⑧[   ] of the idea, however, have ⑨[   ] that it might be difficult to implement in the US, where many people live in ⑩[   ] suburbs and depend on cars for daily life.

Chapter 5

Tiny Houses

持ち物を減らしてシンプルな生活を送る「ミニマリスト」が注目を集めています。アメリカではその方法のひとつとして小さな家に住む「スモールハウス運動」が生まれました。快適で充実した生活を送るために必要なものは何でしょう。

Before You Read

Complete the sentences below.

1. A tiny house has a floor area of 37 square meters or [more / less].
2. In a tiny house, furniture must be [multi-functional / for one use only].
3. If we live in a very small space, privacy must be [established / sacrificed].
4. The expression "empty-nesters" refers to couples whose children [have left home / are living at home].
5. Tiny houses must comply with construction [preferences / regulations].

Moving to Minimalism

1 In 1999, a man in the U.S. state of Wisconsin called Jay Shafer built a tiny house on wheels for himself. It had a floor area of just 10 square meters, yet he lived in it for five years. Later, he produced the first plans for tiny houses on wheels and went on to found companies that built them, as well as a society to promote this type of living. This gave birth to the Small House Movement. The timing for such a development was right. As the popularity of the **minimalist** approach to life shows, more and more people are becoming **attuned to** the idea of living more simply with fewer possessions. Living in a small house potentially offers a way to **put** the idea of simpler living **into practice**.

2 For Japanese people, who are accustomed to relatively small living spaces, it might **come as a shock** to discover that in 2021, the size of the average American family home was around 230 square meters. The small house movement advocated a return to houses of less than 93 square meters. **Subsequently**, the idea of the tiny house — one with a floor area of 37 square meters or less — was developed.

3 But for me at least, living in a tiny house is not an optimal solution. In opting to **downscale** my living accommodations so drastically, the first hurdle I would need to overcome is adapting to an extremely confined living space. For example, I would have to reduce my possessions to the absolute minimum and sacrifice my privacy. This simpler kind of lifestyle might suit retirees or couples whose children have grown up and moved out — so-called

Vocabulary

minimalist
最小主義（者）

attuned to ~
〜に同調している

put ~ into practice
〜を実践する

come as a shock
ショックを与える

subsequently その後

downscale ~
〜を小型化する

empty-nesters. For me, however, it is not an option, as I am married with two young children, and a family needs more space than a tiny house can provide.

4   Like Jay Shafer's original small home, some tiny houses are built on wheels, which means they can be considered as mobile homes and moved from place to place. However, for people who want to settle in one place in a tiny home, there are various obstacles. A tiny home may cost less to build than a **conventional** home, but the land on which it stands must also be purchased. And even if people can afford to do this, they may run into difficulties with **zoning laws**. In many places, tiny houses do not comply with construction regulations that specify the minimum size of a structure.

5   Nevertheless, people are continuing to come up with creative ways to **get around** such problems. Even though living in a tiny house is not a step I would take right now, I am grateful to the small house movement for making people reconsider what we need to lead a comfortable and fulfilling life.

---

empty-nester
子どもが自立して巣立った親

conventional 従来の

zoning law 都市計画法

get around ~
～を上手に回避する

Test Yourself

A Overview

Read the passage and choose the correct statement from each pair.

1. a) Jay Shafer built a tiny house after founding the Small House Movement.
   b) The Small House Movement was established after Jay Shafer built his tiny house.

2. a) Small houses offer people the chance to live in a more environmentally friendly way.
   b) Building small houses is part of the U.S. government's environmental policy.

3. a) Tiny houses often appeal to people in the later stages of life.
   b) Tiny houses are ideal for young couples with children.

4. a) A tiny house and a mobile home are two terms that mean the same thing.
   b) Some tiny houses are very similar to mobile homes.

5. a) Tiny houses often do not comply with rules that specify the size of a structure.
   b) Construction regulations usually allow people to build tiny homes quite easily.

B Focus on Details

Read the passage again and complete each sentence.

1. Jay Shafer _____ companies that produced tiny houses.
   a) found   b) finds   c) founded   d) finding

2. More and more people have adopted the idea of living with _____ possessions.
   a) fewer   b) fewest   c) lesser   d) least

3. It came _____ a shock to me to see how large American homes are.
   a) with   b) for   c) by   d) as

4. Small houses can make life difficult when you are _____ up children.
   a) rising   b) rearing   c) bringing   d) leading

5. A tiny house costs less to build than a _____ house
   a) contemporary   b) convenient   c) conventional   d) continuous

Chapter 5　Tiny Houses

Follow-up

A Zoom In

プレ・リーディング 3：関連語彙をスキャニングする

リーディングにおける「**スキャニング**」（検索読み）とは文章をすばやく、ざっと見て特定の情報を探す作業を言います。概して英文にはタイトルが付属しますが、それをヒントに関連する語彙を検索（スキャング）します。語彙をスキャンする際は以下を念頭におきましょう。

- タイトルに関連するのはどんな語彙か
- その語彙に付随するのはどんな語句か

タイトル Moving to Minimalism から「〜への移行」と「ミニマリズム（最小主義）」というキーワードを念頭に英文をスキャンしていくと、第1パラグラフでは tiny house（小さい家）、living more simply（よりシンプルな暮らし）、more and more people are becoming attuned to 〜（ますます多くの人が〜に賛成している）といった関連する語句が見つかります。この章の英文であれば第1パラグラフのスキャニングだけでも、Moving to Minimalism が「より小さい家でシンプルに生活する考え方に同調する人が増えている」を意味することがわかります。スキャニングの効果を理解するために、タイトルを隠して冒頭から読んでみてください。重視すべき情報がわからず不安になるのではないでしょうか。

B Discussion

Discuss the following statements or questions.

1. What are the benefits and drawbacks of the small house movement?

2. Discuss ideas about leading a simple life other than living in a small house.

Chapter 5　Tiny Houses

A Build Your Vocabulary

Find the words in the reading passage that match the definitions below.

1. (line 6) to help something to develop = _____
2. (line 11) something that belongs to you = _____
3. (line 13) familiar with something = _____
4. (line 17) to publicly support = _____
5. (line 22) most favorable or desirable = _____
6. (line 24) small or limited = _____
7. (line 41) to act as requested = _____
8. (line 48) satisfying or rewarding = _____

B Summary & Dictation

 32

Complete the paragraph with the words below. Change the word form if necessary. Listen to the passage to check the answers.

| • embrace | • adapt | • possession | • minimum | • regulation |
| • sacrifice | • obstacle | • minimalist | • settle | • idea |

As the popularity of the ①[　　　　　　] approach to life shows, more people are thinking about living with fewer ②[　　　　　　]. Living in a small house allows people to put the ③[　　　　　　] of simpler living into practice. Tiny houses have a floor area of 37 square meters or less. But living in a tiny house means ④[　　　　　　] to a confined living space. Furniture must be multi-functional, possessions must be reduced to the ⑤[　　　　　　], and privacy must be ⑥[　　　　　　]. Many retirees have ⑦[　　　　　　] this style of living, but younger couples may find limited space is a problem when bringing up children. Some tiny houses are built on wheels, which means they can be moved from place to place. However, for people who want to ⑧[　　　　　　] in one place, there are ⑨[　　　　　　]. A tiny home may cost less to build than a conventional home, but the land on which it stands must also be purchased and there can be difficulties with construction ⑩[　　　　　　].

Chapter 6 Powering Our Homes

ガスコンロは広く普及していますが、使用時に発生する有害な二酸化窒素についてはあまり知られていません。アメリカではガス器具の使用は徐々に禁止され、IH 調理器のような代替品が使われ始めています。IH 調理器には、どのような長所や問題点があるのでしょうか。

Before You Read

Complete the sentences below.

1. Nitrogen dioxide is [beneficial / harmful] to human health.
2. Gas stoves are a [common / rare] source of harmful substances.
3. Cooking with gas [is linked to / has no connection with] cases of asthma.
4. Using electric induction cookers led to a [significant / negligible] rise in nitrogen dioxide levels.
5. Induction cooking is steadily being [embraced / rejected] by top chefs and restaurants.

Saying Goodbye to Gas

1 Nitrogen dioxide (NO_2) is a gas that is harmful to human health. Long-term exposure to it can worsen conditions such as **asthma** and lung disease, and it can increase the risk of people developing lung or **cardiovascular** disease. It is considered so potentially hazardous that authorities in many countries have set limits to the amount that people can be exposed to when out of doors. We should therefore ask ourselves why we continue to generate unsafe levels of NO_2 **every time** we turn on our gas stoves at home.

2 Evidence emerged that gas stoves are a major source of NO_2 during a recent survey conducted in a public housing building in New York City. It found that in homes with gas stoves, the level of NO_2 increased from a **baseline** level of 18 parts per billion (ppb) to an average of 197ppb during cooking, a figure that greatly exceeded the limit set for safe exposure outdoors. What is more, gas stoves have been linked to one-eighth of all cases of asthma in the US. And **aside from** risks to human health, there are environmental concerns. Methane is a greenhouse gas with a global warming potential 25 times that of carbon dioxide, yet gas stoves emit methane even when they are turned off. Added to that, when we use gas, there is always the possibility of a gas leak or even a gas-**triggered** fire or explosion.

3 Recently, the US Consumer Product Safety Commission announced that it would consider banning gas stoves. So, perhaps **it is high time** we seriously considered switching from gas to electricity, a much cleaner method

that is better for our health and for the environment. As
evidence of this, the New York City survey mentioned
above found that using an **electric induction** stove resulted
in a negligible increase in NO_2 levels, from 11ppb to just
14ppb.

4 Cooking using induction technology, which is
steadily being **embraced** by numerous professional chefs
and a growing number of restaurants, **may well** be the
way of the future. Unlike either gas or conventional
electric cooking, induction technology does not create
heat on the stovetop. Instead, it induces an **electromagnetic**
current directly into the cookware. Not only does this
method not create **pollutants**, it is also much more energy-
efficient. What is more, because the stove itself is not
heated to a high temperature, it cools down very
quickly, thus reducing the risk of accidents.

5 **Admittedly**, not everyone will be able to convert to
induction cooking, partly because of the costs involved.
New stoves must be purchased, and pots made out of
materials that do not conduct electricity, such as copper or
aluminum, must be replaced. But around the world, an
increasing number of towns and cities are deciding that
newly built residential units will no longer have gas **hook-
ups**. It could be that we are witnessing the end of the gas-
cooking age.

electric induction
電気誘導

embrace ~
~を採用する、活用する
may well ~
おそらく~だろう

electromagnetic
電磁気の

pollutant 汚染物質

admittedly 明らかに

hook-up 配管設備

 Test Yourself

A Overview

Read the passage and choose the correct statement from each pair.

1. a) Exposure to NO_2 causes immediate damage to people's health.
   b) NO_2 exposure over long periods is a risk to human health.

2. a) Many countries have already set safety limits for exposure to NO_2.
   b) Several countries are considering passing laws to ban NO_2 exposure.

3. a) Gas stoves emit unsafe levels of methane while in use.
   b) Gas stoves emit a greenhouse gas even when they are not being used.

4. a) Induction stovetops do not get as hot as gas stovetops.
   b) Induction cooking does not heat cookware as much as gas cooking does.

5. a) Lack of public understanding will limit the adoption of induction cooking.
   b) The cost of switching to induction cooking may make it unattractive for some people.

B Focus on Details

Read the passage again and complete each sentence.

1. Long-_____ exposure to NO_2 can cause health problems or make them worse.
   a) year   b) period   c) term   d) lived

2. _____ from risks to human health, there are concerns about environmental damage.
   a) Except   b) Addition   c) As well   d) Aside

3. Using an induction stove resulted _____ a negligible rise in NO_2 levels.
   a) from   b) in   c) with   d) about

4. Induction cooking is steadily being embraced by a _____ number of restaurants.
   a) grown   b) grow   c) growing   d) grew

5. Switching to induction technology _____ well be the way of the future.
   a) will   b) would   c) should   d) may

42

Chapter 6　Powering Our Homes

A　Zoom In

プレ・リーディング 4：パラグラフ冒頭をスキミングする

語彙や文法の理解に重点をおかず、文章にざっと目を通して概要をつかむことを「**スキミング**」（概略読み）と言います。多くの場合、以下のように各パラグラフの最初の文（主題文）をスキミングすることにより英文全体の論旨を把握できます。

> 第1パラグラフ「二酸化炭素は健康に有害なガスだ」
> 第2パラグラフ「二酸化炭素の主な発生源はガスストーブだと調査で判明した」
> 第3パラグラフ「アメリカのある委員会がガスストーブの使用禁止を検討する予定」
> 第4パラグラフ「ある技術を活用した料理法が将来の活路になるだろう」
> 第5パラグラフ「コスト面から誰もがその料理法に転換できるわけではない」

主題文であるため具体的な情報は含まれないですが、英文全体の要点を理解するには十分です。マラソン選手が試走してコース点検するように、スキャニングの目的は英文中の目印を見つけ、全体の展開を予測することにあります。

B　Discussion

Discuss the following statements or questions.

1. What type of cooking stove do you have in your house? What are its advantages and disadvantages?

2. Besides gas-cooking stoves, what appliances do you think may be replaced in the near future? How?

Chapter 6   Powering Our Homes

A Build Your Vocabulary

Find the words in the reading passage that match the definitions below.

1. (line 2) having no protection from something harmful = _____
2. (line 6) dangerous, risky = _____
3. (line 16) to go or be beyond = _____
4. (line 22) to send out, release = _____
5. (line 32) too small to be considered or worried about = _____
6. (line 45) to change = _____
7. (line 49) to take the place of something = _____
8. (line 52) to see something happen = _____

B Summary & Dictation

 38

Complete the paragraph with the words below. Change the word form if necessary. Listen to the passage to check the answers.

| • witness | • conduct | • induce | • greenhouse | • hazardous |
| • pollutant | • convert | • residential | • switch | • limit |

Long-term exposure to NO_2 is harmful to human health. It is so potentially ①[   ] that authorities in many countries have set safety ②[   ]. There are also environmental concerns. Gas stoves emit methane, a ③[   ] gas, even when they are turned off. Perhaps it is high time we seriously considered ④[   ] from gas to induction technology, a much cleaner method of cooking. It does not create heat on the stovetop. Instead, it ⑤[   ] an electromagnetic current directly into the cookware. This method does not create ⑥[   ] and is more energy-efficient. Not everyone will be able to ⑦[   ] to induction cooking, partly because of the costs involved. New stoves must be purchased, and pots made out of materials that do not ⑧[   ] electricity must be replaced. Around the world, more towns and cities are no longer installing gas hook-ups in newly built ⑨[   ] units. Perhaps we are ⑩[   ] the end of the gas-cooking age.

Chapter 7

The Future of Cars

従来、自動車は自由さや気楽さを求めて購入するものでしたが、近年は大きく変わりつつあります。自由さや気楽さを求める時代は終わったのでしょうか。自動車を所有することのメリットとデメリットは何でしょう。なぜ変わってしまったのでしょう。

Before You Read

Complete the sentences below.

1. The era [preceding / following] World War II is known as the golden age of the automobile.
2. The year 2006 marked a [boom / turning point] in car ownership.
3. The number of people [over / under] the age of 34 who have driver's licenses is declining.
4. Having a car could be considered a [necessity / luxury] for people living in the suburbs or the countryside.
5. For many people nowadays, cars no longer represent [freedom / a burden].

Cars — Who Needs Them?

1 If I had to choose one factor that has influenced the way we live more than any other, I would say it is the development of automobile culture, which has shaped our living environment and even our lives **as a whole**.

2 Ever since 1908, when the Ford Motor Company introduced the Model T, the world's first **affordable**, mass-produced automobile, cars have held a symbolic place in our modern culture. Initially, they symbolized a move away from a pre-industrial age into a dynamic and fast-paced new world fueled by technology. By the post-World War II era, they had come to represent independence and freedom. A fall in prices, a boom in manufacturing, and the **massive** development of road infrastructure all led to the golden age of the automobile.

3 Acquiring a driver's license and getting one's first car was seen as a **rite of passage** from childhood into adulthood. **Accordingly**, throughout the 20th century, there was a boom in car ownership and the number of driver's licenses issued. But in 2006, something changed. Since then, the number of registered vehicles in the U.S. has continued to fall, according to the U.S. Federal Highway Administration. More worryingly for the future of the car industry, research shows that the number of people between the ages of 16 and 34 with driver's licenses is declining steadily. Additionally, among the **millennial generation**, 54 percent said they would consider not owning a car if other forms of transportation were available.

Vocabulary

as a whole 全体的に

affordable 手の届く、手ごろな価格の

massive 大規模な

rite of passage 通過儀礼
accordingly その結果として

millennial generation ミレニアル世代（＝ジェネレーションY）

4　One reason behind this trend could be a change in how cars are perceived. Rather than representing a life of ease, freedom, and independence, cars are starting to be seen as a burden. For example, with rises in the price of fuel, insurance, and maintenance, owning a car is no longer affordable for many people. A car may still be a necessity for people living outside **urban centers**, but for an increasing number of city **dwellers**, improved public transportation systems have eliminated this need.

5　There are two other major factors. The rise of remote working during the COVID-19 pandemic reduced the need for workers to commute into cities, and possibly led to people questioning the value of owning a car. **On top of** this, there are environmental considerations. With their heavy emissions of CO_2, motor vehicles are a major contributor to global warming. Consequently, there is a growing **sentiment** that if we really care about the health of the planet, we should be **opting for** public transportation or less-polluting methods of travel such as bicycles or electric scooters.

6　For better or worse, we have built a car-focused society in which the needs of drivers have been **prioritized**. It would not be a bad thing if we were to rethink our relationship with motor vehicles.

urban center 都心

dweller 住人

on top of ~ ～に加えて

sentiment 感情

opt for ~ ～を選択する

prioritize ~
～を優先する

A Overview

Read the passage and choose the correct statement from each pair.

1. a) Throughout the 20th century, cars came to symbolize freedom and independence.
   b) Throughout the 20th century, cars increasingly came to be seen as a burden rather than a blessing.
2. a) Since 2006, the rate of increase in the number of registered vehicles in the U.S. has slowed down.
   b) Since 2006, the number of registered vehicles in the U.S. has been on the decline.
3. a) Many people no longer have enough money to meet all the various expenses of car ownership.
   b) The rising price of automobiles has discouraged many people from buying one.
4. a) Many people sold their cars after they were forced to stay at home during the COVID-19 pandemic.
   b) Changes in working styles brought about by the COVID-19 pandemic mean there is less need to own a car.
5. a) A majority of the U.S. millennial generation would consider not owning a car if their transportation needs could be met in another way.
   b) The U.S. millennial generation is overwhelmingly opposed to car ownership because of environmental concerns.

B Focus on Details

Read the passage again and complete each sentence.

1. Since the introduction of Ford's Model T, the car has held a _____ place in modern culture.
   a) symbol   b) symbolizing   c) symbolic   d) symbolized
2. By the post-World War II era, cars had _____ to represent freedom and independence.
   a) come   b) become   c) achieved   d) arrived
3. Fifty-four percent of U.S. millennials said they would consider not owning a car if other forms of transportation were _____.
   a) popular   b) common   c) current   d) available
4. Two other major factors play _____ the decline in car ownership.
   a) out of   b) around   c) into   d) with
5. CO_2 emissions from motor vehicles are a major contributor to global warming. _____, we should be opting for less-polluting methods of travel.
   a) However   b) Consequently   c) Fortunately   d) Nevertheless

Chapter 7　The Future of Cars

A Zoom In

ホワイル・リーディング とは

英文読解の際に以下のような質問を「考えながら読解する」ことをホワイル・リーディング（while-reading）と言います。ここでは具体的に以下を行います。

1. 自問自答しながら読む
   理解度を自ら確認しながら読み進める。
2. 事実と意見を区別する
   語彙や表現を元に事実と著者の意見を区別して理解する。
3. 推測・予測する
   述べられていることから推測する。以降の展開を予測しつつ読解する。
4. 注釈を付ける
   読み終えた後の振り返りに備えて注釈を記入する。

この章の英文のように多くの人が背景知識を持つトピックであっても、これらすべて行いながら読解するのは容易なことではありません。重要なのは日本語に訳すことに100%頭を使うのではなく、上記の作業にも脳のリソースを費やしつつ読み下していく姿勢です。

B Discussion

Discuss the following statements or questions.

1. Do you ever want to own a car? Why? Why not?

2. Based on the reading passage, discuss what has changed in commuting to school or work after the COVID-19 pandemic.

Chapter 7 The Future of Cars

Wrap-up

A Build Your Vocabulary

Find the words in the reading passage that match the definitions below.

1. (line 10) to support, stimulate = _____
2. (line 13) the system of public works of a country, city, etc. = _____
3. (line 24) to gradually become smaller = _____
4. (line 26) the means to move people or goods from place to place = _____
5. (line 29) to think of something in a particular way = _____
6. (line 36) to get rid of, remove = _____
7. (line 38) far away from other people, houses, etc. = _____
8. (line 43) something that is partly responsible for something = _____

B Summary & Dictation

 45

Complete the paragraph with the words below. Change the word form if necessary. Listen to the passage to check the answers.

- burden
- independent
- boom
- massive
- suburb
- eliminate
- own
- afford
- insure
- symbol

Ever since the Ford Motor Company introduced the world's first ①[   ], mass-produced automobile in 1908, cars have held a ②[   ] place in modern culture. By the post-World War II era, they had come to represent ③[   ] and freedom. A fall in prices, a ④[   ] in manufacturing, and the ⑤[   ] development of road infrastructure all led to the golden age of the automobile. Throughout the 20th century, there was an explosion in car ⑥[   ]. But from 2006, the number of registered vehicles in the U.S. has continued to fall. Cars no longer represent freedom and independence but are seen by some as a ⑦[   ]. With rises in the price of fuel, ⑧[   ], and maintenance, owning a car is too expensive for many people. A car may still be necessary for people living in the countryside or ⑨[   ], but for city dwellers, improved public transportation systems have ⑩[   ] this need.

Chapter 8

Superhumans

人類は約20万年間、生物学的にほとんど進化していません。しかしながら「トランスヒューマニズム」という主張によると、今後の技術進歩により人間の認知能力は向上し、その結果寿命が延びるとされます。どのような根拠に基づく主張なのでしょう。

Before You Read

Complete the sentences below.

1. Generally speaking, the evolution of species proceeds at a very [slow / rapid] pace.
2. Human beings are extremely [likely / unlikely] to experience rapid biological changes in the near future.
3. The term "transhumanism" suggests [staying within / going beyond] the current limits of being human.
4. Nanobots are [microscopic / enormous] robots that could play a major role in future health care.
5. It would be foolish to [reject / embrace] the idea that incredible leaps in technological progress are quite possible.

Leaving Our Old Selves Behind

1 When we compare ourselves to our earliest pre-human ancestors, it is clear how much we have evolved as a species. But evolution moves at an unimaginably slow pace. Since the emergence of homo sapiens around 200,000 years ago, we have not undergone significant biological changes, and we are unlikely to experience any in the near future. We have indeed evolved, but the changes have been **predominantly** cultural and technological, not biological. But given how rapidly various areas of technology are developing, it is logical to assume that physical and cognitive **enhancement** through technology is likely to be the next great step in human evolution.

2 This idea is **embodied** in an exciting new school of thought known as "transhumanism." As the name suggests, transhumanism is centered around a belief that we can go beyond being mere humans. **Proponents** say that this can be achieved with the aid of current technologies such as genetic engineering and information technology as well as anticipated advances in others such as bioengineering, artificial intelligence, and nanotechnology.

3 One of the leading thinkers in this movement who I admire is Dr. Ray Kurzweil, a renowned AI visionary and inventor of **cutting-edge** technologies. Despite acknowledging the current challenges human beings face, such as climate change, environmental **degradation**, economic inequality, and armed conflict, Kurzweil is optimistic about the future of the human race. He has often written about an event he calls the Singularity. According to

Kurzweil, this refers to a point in the future when the
30 **exponential** progress of technology and AI becomes so
great that it fundamentally changes human beings and our
civilization. He envisions a future in which we will
transcend our current limitations by **merging with**
intelligent machines, resulting in enhanced cognitive
35 abilities and an increased lifespan.

4   Some of his predictions seem taken directly from
the pages of science-fiction stories. For instance, he
foresees neural implants that will make it possible for
our brains to communicate directly with computers.
40 **On the** health **front**, he has written about **microscopic**
robots (nanobots) that can be inserted into our bodies to
repair damage to cells and potentially slow the aging
process. But his most fantastic and controversial assertion
is that human consciousness can be digitized and uploaded
45 onto a computer, potentially making it possible for people
to survive the death of their body. Kurzweil has even given
a date to his predictions: he says the Singularity could be
here as early as 2045.

5   Predictably, many scientists are too **short-sighted**
50 to appreciate these revolutionary new ideas. They hotly
dispute Kurzweil's predictions and assertions, finding
them too **far-fetched** to take seriously. However, I stand
behind Kurzweil. **Given** the astounding technological
leaps we have made from the beginning of the 20th
55 century, we are surely correct to put our faith in
transhumanism as the best hope for a bright future.

---

exponential 飛躍的な

merge with ~
～と融合する

on the ~ front
～の分野において
microscopic 極小の

short-sighted
近視眼的な

far-fetched
実現しそうにない
given~ ～を考慮すると

 Test Yourself

A Overview

Read the passage and choose the correct statement from each pair.

1. a) It is clear to see how much present-day humans have evolved from their primitive ancestors.
   b) Present-day human beings have not evolved very much from our early hominid ancestors.
2. a) The near future is likely to see human beings undergoing profound biological changes changes.
   b) Any human evolution in the near future is likely to be technological and cultural rather than biological.
3. a) Proponents of transhumanism believe human beings will naturally evolve to go beyond our current limits.
   b) Transhumanists believe that human beings will evolve with the aid of cutting-edge technologies.
4. a) Kurzweil believes that human consciousness can be preserved through the use of nanobots.
   b) Kurzweil believes that human consciousness could be digitized and preserved as computer data.
5. a) Kurzweil's ideas on humanity's future are not considered favorably by other scientists.
   b) Other scientists generally accept Kurzweil's predictions for the future of humanity.

B Focus on Details

Read the passage again and complete each sentence.

1. If we _____ homo sapiens to its early ancestors, we can see how much the species has evolved.
   a) will compare   b) compare   c) compared   d) had compared
2. We are extremely _____ to undergo large-scale biological evolution in the near future.
   a) improbable   b) impossible   c) unreasonable   d) unlikely
3. Transhumanism is based on the belief that we can go _____ the limits of being human.
   a) beyond   b) around   c) against   d) until
4. Kurzweil has _____ changes that seem to come from the pages of science fiction stories.
   a) premeditated   b) previewed   c) predicted   d) prepared
5. Kurzweil has said that technology will make it possible for people _____ beyond the death of the body.
   a) survive   b) to survive   c) surviving   d) survived

Chapter 8　Superhumans

A Zoom In

ホワイル・リーディング1：自問自答しながら読む

ホワイル・リーディングの基本は「**自問自答しながら読む**」ことです。ひとつの文や長い節を読み終えたら立ち止まって以下の質問を自分に問いかけ、確認しながら読み下していきます。

- 英文内容を正しく理解できて（訳せて）いるか
- 重要と思われるキーワードを読み飛ばしていないか
- 著者の主張を順に追って理解できているか
- 話の流れに論理的な矛盾（論理の飛躍など）はないか

本章の英文を例にとると、まずは第2パラグラフの "transhumanism" というキーワードを確実におさえます。次に、transhumanism を念頭に置いて第4パラグラフまで順を追って疑問を持ちつつ批判的に読解していきます。最後に第5パラグラフにある However, I stand behind Kurzweil. と we are surely correct to... という著者の主張を踏まえ、前段までの内容と論理的矛盾がないことを確認するという手順です。自分の理解度を確認しつつ、内容を疑いつつ、最後まで興味を維持しつつ読み進めましょう。

B Discussion

Discuss the following statements or questions.

1. What do you think is the most astounding technological advancement in history? How does it affect our daily lives?

2. Based on the idea of transhumanism, do you think humans can evolve even further? Why? How?

Chapter 8 Superhumans

A Build Your Vocabulary

Find the words in the reading passage that match the definitions below.

1. (line 4) the act or process of coming into existence = _____
2. (line 19) expected, predicted or foreseen = _____
3. (line 22) highly honored or celebrated = _____
4. (line 26) a serious disagreement = _____
5. (line 33) to go beyond the limits of something = _____
6. (line 42) possibly but not yet actually = _____
7. (line 51) to argue about something = _____
8. (line 53) very surprising or amazing = _____

B Summary & Dictation

Complete the paragraph with the words below. Change the word form if necessary. Listen to the passage to check the answers.

- implant • beyond • enhance • direct • envision
- process • survive • insert • fundamental • cognitive

Physical and cognitive ①[   ] through technology is likely to be the next great step in human evolution. Transhumanism is the belief that we can go ②[   ] being mere humans by using genetic engineering, information technology, bioengineering, artificial intelligence, and nanotechnology. Dr. Ray Kurzweil has written about a point in the future when the progress of technology and AI becomes so great that it ③[   ] changes human beings. He ④[   ] a future in which we will merge with intelligent machines, resulting in enhanced ⑤[   ] abilities and an increased lifespan. He foresees neural ⑥[   ] that will make it possible for our brains to communicate ⑦[   ] with computers, or nanobots that can be ⑧[   ] into our bodies to repair cell damage and slow the aging ⑨[   ]. He also asserts that human consciousness can be digitized and uploaded onto a computer, making it possible for people to ⑩[   ] bodily death.

56

Chapter 9 Restaurants in Crisis

誰しも憧れる豪華な最高級料理を最上級の快適さで提供する超高級レストランですが、時としてそこで働く人々の労働環境は煌びやかな雰囲気とはかけ離れたものです。食事客が支払う高額な料金を踏まえると理解し難いことですが、背後には何があるのでしょう。

Before You Read

Complete the sentences below.

1. Working conditions for kitchen staff in high-class restaurants are usually very [attractive / demanding].
2. Recently, programs about the realities of restaurant work have become [popular / rare] on television.
3. Noma, a restaurant in [Copenhagen / Paris], has been top of the World's Best 50 Restaurants list five times.
4. [Despite / Because of] its high prices, Noma has faced a financial struggle.
5. High-end restaurants found it [easy / difficult] to adapt to the changes brought about by the COVID-19 pandemic.

Kitchen Staff — Workers or Slaves?

1   In a top-class restaurant, the sky-high price tag is a guarantee that the dining experience will be smooth, luxurious, and stress-free. But my enjoyment of the meal is immediately spoiled when I think of the kitchen, where low-paid workers **toil** under enormous pressure amid shouting and bullying from senior staff. Until recently, these working conditions were unknown to outsiders. But with an **upsurge** of interest in restaurants, driven by the emergence of so-called celebrity chefs and popular TV programs about the harsh realities of restaurant work, the lid has been lifted to reveal a **toxic** and abusive working culture. In fact, in a report on the restaurant industry in 2017, the Washington Post found that even physical assault and sexual harassment were not uncommon in restaurant kitchens.

2   In January 2023, the restaurant world was shaken by the news that the restaurant Noma, in the Danish capital of Copenhagen, would shut down at the end of 2024. For nearly 15 years, Noma has been considered the world's most influential restaurant, winning the top spot on the list of the World's Best 50 Restaurants five times. In announcing the closure, Noma's chef and owner, René Redzepi, said he had taken the decision because he found that running a restaurant **dedicated to** fine dining was "unsustainable" emotionally and financially.

3   In 2021, the average price **per head** for one of Noma's course meals was around $500, so I found it hard to believe that the restaurant faced a financial struggle. But as I later discovered, creating high-level food at **top-tier** restaurants

Vocabulary

toil あくせく働く

upsurge 急激な高まり

toxic 心身を蝕（むしば）む

dedicate ~ to ... ～を…にささげる

per head 1人当たり

top-tier 最上階

requires enormous effort. Noma was only able to succeed
thanks to a large number of interns. These young people
are prepared to put up with the abusive conditions while
working **punishingly** long hours in return for a **meager
paycheck** (or even no money at all!) because they hope
that their experience will launch them into a better-paid
position elsewhere.

4 **To his credit**, Redzepi has admitted bullying his
staff both verbally and physically. His decision to close
Noma is a symptom of a wider realization among the
public and restaurant professionals that the current
business model of top-tier restaurants must change
because it is both abusive and **exploitative**.

5 As in many other **spheres**, the effects of the
COVID-19 pandemic are accelerating changes. It is not
surprising that the restaurants that suffered most in the
pandemic were **fine-dining** establishments, because they
were unable to **pivot** rapidly **to** the new conditions, including
demand for simpler take-out or delivery meals. And as
awareness grows of just how badly younger staff are
treated, we can perhaps hope that the restaurant industry
will find a more **humane** way to move forward.

Test Yourself

A Overview

Read the passage and choose the correct statement from each pair.

1. a) The harsh working conditions in restaurant kitchens have only recently become widely known.
   b) We have known for a long time that staff in restaurant kitchens experience tough and even abusive working conditions.
2. a) Noma in Copenhagen is one of the world's most profitable restaurants.
   b) The restaurant Noma in Copenhagen can be considered one of the world's top restaurants.
3. a) Young interns at Noma have been willing to tolerate long hours and low pay in the hope of future rewards.
   b) Young interns at Noma went on strike to protest against low pay and abusive working conditions.
4. a) The owner of Noma has rejected claims that he bullied his staff both verbally and physically.
   b) The owner of Noma has stated that he regrets treating his staff abusively.
5. a) In order to survive during the COVID-19 pandemic, restaurants had to switch to providing take-out or delivery meals.
   b) Fine-dining establishments were among the most successful restaurants during the COVID-19 pandemic.

B Focus on Details

Read the passage again and complete each sentence.

1. In _____ restaurants, low-paid workers work under enormous pressure amid shouting and bullying from senior kitchen staff.
   a) almost   b) most of   c) all of   d) almost all
2. The restaurant Noma in Copenhagen announced that it would shut _____ at the end of 2024.
   a) up   b) down   c) in   d) out
3. _____ that the price for one of Noma's course meals is around $500, it is hard to believe that the restaurant faced a financial struggle.
   a) Considered   b) Considering   c) Consider   d) Consideration
4. Redzepi has admitted _____ his staff both verbally and physically
   a) bullying   b) to bully   c) bullied   d) bullies
5. Young interns are prepared to put up _____ low pay and long hours in return for future rewards.
   a) from   b) with   c) along   d) about

Chapter 9　Restaurants in Crisis

A　Zoom In

ホワイル・リーディング 2：事実と意見を区別する

書かれている内容に関して「**事実と意見を区別する**」ことは批判的読解における必須のスキルです。事実とは異なり、著者の意見は批判の対象（意義を唱える余地がある）となるため注意深く読解します。著者の考えや意見はしばしば以下のような語彙やフレーズとともに提示されます。

- I think / find . . .（私は〜と思う）
- in my opinion / view . . .（私の意見・見解では〜）
- it seems to me that . . .（私には〜と思える）
- it is likely that . . .（おそらく〜だろう）
- we may conclude that . . .（〜と結論づけてもよいだろう）

本章の英文では、第3パラグラフの I found it hard to . . .（〜が難しいと思った）、第5パラグラフの It is not surprising that . . .（〜は驚くようなことではない）、we can perhaps hope that . . .（ひょっとしたら〜を期待することができる）の後に著者の意見や考えが述べられています。

B　Discussion

Discuss the following statements or questions.

1. Discuss the features (e.g., menu, atmosphere, location) that high-class restaurants in Japan share. How important are they to the customers?

2. Other than the restaurant industry, what field suffered greatly from the effects of COVID 19? How has it changed afterward?

61

A Build Your Vocabulary

Find the words in the reading passage that match the definitions below.

1. (line 3) very comfortable and expensive = _____
2. (line 5) very great in amount or degree = _____
3. (line 11) involving physical or emotional violence = _____
4. (line 13) a violent attack = _____
5. (line 27) a long effort to deal with something difficult = _____
6. (line 38) a sign or indication of something = _____
7. (line 43) to cause to happen sooner = _____
8. (line 48) knowing that something exists = _____

B Summary & Dictation

 57

Complete the paragraph with the words below. Change the word form if necessary. Listen to the passage to check the answers.

| •finance | •sustain | •emotion | •announce | •require |
| •realize | •prepare | •influence | •decide | •abuse |

In January 2023, the restaurant Noma in Copenhagen ①[   ] it would shut down. For nearly 15 years, Noma has been considered the world's most ②[   ] restaurant, topping the list of the World's Best 50 Restaurants five times. Noma's chef and owner said he had taken the decision because he found that running the restaurant was ③[   ] both ④[   ] and financially. Considering that the price for one of Noma's course meals is around $500, it might be hard to believe that the restaurant faced a ⑤[   ] struggle. But creating food at such a high level ⑥[   ] an enormous amount of work. Noma was able to be financially stable thanks to a large number of young interns, who are ⑦[   ] to put up with ⑧[   ] conditions and long hours because they hope their experience will benefit them in the future. Redzepi's ⑨[   ] to close Noma is perhaps a ⑩[   ] that the current business model of top-tier restaurants must change.

Chapter 10: Lab-grown Meat

倫理的な観点や健康面で肉類を食べない人が増えていますが、その風味や食感を好む人がいる限り、すべての人がベジタリアンやビーガンへと転換するのは事実上ありえないことです。どちらの立場の人も満足させる方法はないのでしょうか。

Before You Read

Complete the sentences below.

1. [More / Less] than 30 percent of India's population identifies as vegetarian.
2. The number of people who oppose a meat-based diet is currently [growing / diminishing].
3. So-called "vegan meat" has been [popular / available] since the 1950s.
4. Meat can be grown in laboratories by extracting [proteins / stem cells] from muscle tissue.
5. In the near future, meat is likely to [disappear from / remain part of] our diets.

 Reading Passage 58~62

Better Than the Real Thing?

1   Meat is a major **component** of diets around the world, but do we really need it? I adopted a vegan diet a few years ago, so I know that human beings can certainly **thrive** without it. In fact, a report by a major research firm in 2021 claimed that approximately 28 percent of the global population identifies as vegetarian, including around 39 percent of India's population.

2   We are now witnessing a growing anti-meat **sentiment**. Some people object on ethical grounds, arguing that it is morally wrong to kill animals for food. Others take a more practical view, pointing out that the practice is unsound economically and environmentally. At a rough estimate, we **derive** just 18 percent of our calories and 37 percent of our protein **from** meat and dairy products. Yet producing them requires an astounding 83 percent of the world's farmland and **accounts for** 60 percent of greenhouse emissions from the agricultural sector.

3   Even though, like me, an increasing number of people are becoming vegetarian or vegan, meat still forms a major part of many people's diet. Partly this is **out of habit**, but at the same time people enjoy the taste and texture of meat and would feel deprived if it was absent from their meals. So, rather than trying to persuade people to give it up, a more practical solution might be to **come up with** a substitute.

4   Since the 1950s, it has been possible to produce so-called "vegan meat" from a mixture of soya, wheat gluten,

Vocabulary
component 一部を成すもの
thrive（健康的に）育つ
sentiment 感情、意見
derive ~ from . . . …から~を得る
account for ~ ~（の割合）を占める
out of habit 習慣で
come up with ~ ~を考え出す

and vegetables. The taste and texture, however, are no match for real meat, and so it has failed to **catch on**. A
more promising approach may be high-tech efforts to scientifically "grow" meat in laboratories. This can be done by extracting stem cells from animals' **muscle tissue** and **culturing** them with **nutrients** and growth-promoting chemicals. After a time, this process can generate enough
cells to form small strips of muscle. These strips can then be combined to form larger pieces of meat. Unfortunately, the technology does not yet exist to use this method to produce larger chunks of meat like steaks. But it can produce what looks like ground meat. This was used to
make the world's first **lab-grown** burger in 2015, which won praise from some food critics.

5　　Scientists are working hard to produce more authentic-seeming meat. But even if they succeed, we will still lack the technology necessary to **put** any new method
into mass production. Additionally, in the light of the negative reaction to genetically modified food, people **may well** be reluctant to accept meat grown in the laboratory as a safe substitute for real meat. It therefore seems reasonable to assume that unless the world
undergoes a mass **conversion to** vegetarianism, which unfortunately seems highly unlikely, meat will still be on our tables for a long time to come.

A Overview

Read the passage and choose the correct statement from each pair.

1. a) Human beings find it hard to thrive without meat in their diet.
   b) Human beings seem able to live well without consuming meat.
2. a) There are both moral and practical reasons for not eating meat.
   b) Most people opposed to eating meat object to it on ethical grounds.
3. a) "Vegan meat" has been available for a long time but has not caught on.
   b) Scientists are hopeful of producing the first "vegan meat" in the near future.
4. a) Lab-grown burgers have been widely available since 2015.
   b) The world's first lab-grown burger found favor with some food critics.
5. a) The biggest barrier to producing artificial meat is the lack of technology to mass-produce it.
   b) It seems unlikely that scientists will ever produce lab-grown meat with authentic taste and texture.

B Focus on Details

Read the passage again and complete each sentence.

1. A report claimed that around 28 percent of the global population _____ as vegetarian
    a) identifies b) regards c) calls d) claims

2. Some people take an ethical stance, _____ that it is morally wrong to kill animals to provide food
    a) argue b) arguing c) arguably d) argument

3. Producing meat and dairy products accounts _____ 60 percent of greenhouse emissions from agriculture.
    a) for b) in c) with d) on

4. Meat can be "grown" by _____ stem cells from muscle tissue and culturing them with nutrients.
    a) expelling b) excluding c) extracting d) expressing

5. _____ there is a mass conversion to vegetarianism, meat will still be on our tables for a long time to come
    a) Although b) Because c) Before d) Unless

Chapter 10　Lab-grown Meat

A Zoom In

ホワイル・リーディング3：推測・予測する

書かれている情報を正しく理解するのは当然として、その時点で述べられていない情報を「**推論・予測する**」ことは批判的読解には欠かせない手順です。英文を読む際は、著者と対峙するような心構えで明示的に伝えられない事柄を推論し、既読内容と照らし合わせて以降の流れを予測します。推論・予測する際には以下について考えましょう。

- 著者の主張は明確か
- 提示された情報から何が推測できるか
- 既読内容から以降どのような展開になると考えられるか
- どのような結論が予測できるか

この章の英文では最初のパラグラフで著者は読者に but do we really need it? と食肉の必要性を問いかけていることから、以降は賛否両方の見解が提示されると推測できます。意見が割れるトピックのため結論を下すのは難しいのではと予測できるかも知れません。実際に以降は議論が提示され、最終的に It therefore seems reasonable to assume that . . .（したがって〜と考えるのが合理的と思われる）と著者は控え目に結論を述べています。

B Discussion

Discuss the following statements or questions.

1. Are you for or against eating no meat at all? Why?

2. Would you give up on eating real meat if a perfect meat substitute should be generated and sold in the supermarket?

Chapter 10   Lab-grown Meat

A Build Your Vocabulary

Find the words in the reading passage that match the definitions below.

1. (line 5) to assert that something is true = _____
2. (line 12) not acceptable = _____
3. (line 22) to take a way something necessary = _____
4. (line 25) a thing serving in place of another = _____
5. (line 30) likely to be successful = _____
6. (line 32) to take out something = _____
7. (line 41) a person who expresses an unfavorable opinion = _____
8. (line 50) to pass through something necessary = _____

B Summary & Dictation

Complete the paragraph with the words below. Change the word form if necessary. Listen to the passage to check the answers.

| • catch on | • sound | • persuade | • extract | • opponent |
| • lack | • texture | • promise | • nutrient | • deprive |

Some ①[   ] of eating meat argue that it is morally wrong to kill animals for food. Others point out that the practice is ②[   ] from an economic and environmental standpoint. But people enjoy the taste and texture of meat and would feel ③[   ] if it were no longer part of their meals. So, rather than ④[   ] people to give it up, it is a better idea to come up with a substitute. Since the 1950s, it has been possible to produce so-called "vegan meat." The taste and ⑤[   ], however, are no match for real meat, and so it has failed to ⑥[   ]. A more ⑦[   ] approach may be to scientifically "grow" meat in laboratories by ⑧[   ] stem cells from muscle tissue and culturing them with ⑨[   ]. Scientists are working hard to produce more authentic-seeming meat. But even if they are successful, we will still ⑩[   ] the technology necessary to put any new method into mass production.

68

Chapter 11

Van Living

近年、生活設備の整った小型トラック（van）で暮らす人が急増しています。若い人たちの中には、ライフスタイルの選択肢として積極的にバンライフを送る人もいますが、背景にはどのような事情があるのでしょう。

Complete the sentences below.

1. In recent years, there has been [an upsurge / a downturn] in people choosing to live in vans.
2. Many social media users post pictures of themselves with their vans in [exotic / familiar] locations.
3. The current economic climate makes it [impossible / easy] for some senior citizens to retire.
4. Some older people drive around the U.S. in search of [seasonal / permanent] employment.
5. The availability of high-speed Internet has [facilitated / complicated] the possibility of long-term living in a van.

69

Reading Passage

Time to Hit the Road

1 Recently, there has been an **upsurge** of people choosing to **renounce** regular forms of accommodation in favor of living in a van that has been **equipped with** basic amenities. This lifestyle is known as "vanliving," "vandwelling," or "vanlife." If you search for "#vanlife" on Instagram, you will find thousands of photos of young and attractive van dwellers posting photos of their life on the road from beaches, mountains, and other attractive locations.

2 These pictures, however, do not tell the full story. Though there may be many who have adopted "vanliving" as a way to pursue their dreams of freedom and adventure, there are many others who have adopted the lifestyle because they had no other choice.

3 The Academy Award winning U.S. movie *Nomadland* (2020) revealed the **plight** of older Americans who lead a **nomadic** van-based lifestyle, not by choice but out of necessity. Compared to other developed countries, the U.S. does not have a generous or comprehensive social safety net. More and more senior citizens find it impossible to retire because they receive little or no income from a **pension** and have no savings. The solution for many of them is to equip a van with basic essentials for long-term living and drive around the country in search of work, such as fruit-picking or fulfilling orders in Amazon's giant warehouses.

4 During the financial crash of 2008 and the subsequent **recession**, many Americans lost almost everything

Vocabulary

upsurge 急増

renounce ~
~を放棄する
equip A with B
AにBを備えつける

plight 苦境
nomadic
放浪する、あちこち移動する

pension 年金

recession 景気後退

they had, including their houses, jobs, and retirement funds. If they were living in an area where jobs were scarce
30 or where accommodation costs were more than they could afford, **taking to the road** in a van offered a solution.

take to the road
旅に出る、車上生活をする

5   Clearly, not all those who live in vans are part of this group, and there are many younger people — even some with young children — who actively **embrace** it **as** a
35 lifestyle choice. With remote working becoming more established as a result of the COVID-19 pandemic and the widespread availability of high-speed Internet service, it is now possible to do **lucrative** work while on the road.

embrace A as B
AをBとして受け入れる

lucrative 実入りの良い

40 **6**   We may conclude that there are two main factors behind people's decisions to adopt "vanlife." One is that lack of financial security gives some people little alternative. Though this lifestyle may have drawbacks, I believe it is a rational response when money and
45 employment opportunities are scarce. The other is a desire for freedom and the attraction of a nomadic life. In my opinion, this is an overly **romantic** view. It seems to me that for most people who adopt this style of living, the novelty will wear off quickly and that they will
50 eventually regret not taking a more conventional path in life.

romantic 非現実的な

A Overview

Read the passage and choose the correct statement from each pair.

1. a) People adopt "vandwelling" as a lifestyle for a number of different reasons.
   b) The term "vandwelling" is limited to families trying out a new kind of lifestyle.
2. a) The U.S. movie *Nomadland* depicted attractive young people traveling by van to exotic locations.
   b) The U.S. movie *Nomadland* depicted older Americans driving around the country in search of work.
3. a) Some senior citizens in the U.S. find it impossible to retire because they lack the money to do so.
   b) The U.S. social safety net provides adequate retirement funds for almost all senior citizens.
4. a) In the U.S. there are many young families driving around looking for seasonal work such as fruit picking.
   b) Common jobs for older Americans living in vans include fruit picking and working in Amazon warehouses.
5. a) Living in a van offers an enjoyable and carefree lifestyle to those who choose to adopt it.
   b) Living in a van may be a sensible lifestyle choice for some people, but others may come to regret it.

B Focus on Details

Read the passage again and complete each sentence.

1. Some people have chosen to _____ regular accommodation in favor of living in a well-equipped van.
   a) renegotiate   b) reform   c) renounce   d) retry
2. _____ many people have adopted "vanliving" a way to pursue freedom, others have done so out of necessity.
   a) Despite   b) Though   c) Even   d) However
3. Some U.S. senior citizens face financial difficulties, having little or no pension income and no savings to fall _____ on.
   a) back   b) over   c) through   d) in
4. The _____ crash of 2008 pushed a lot of people into living in vans.
   a) finance   b) financing   c) financier   d) financial
5. When money and job opportunities are _____, deciding to live in a van is a rational response.
   a) little   b) unusual   c) nothing   d) scarce

Chapter 11　Van Living

A　Zoom In

ホワイル・リーディング 4：注釈を付ける

自問自答しながら事実と意見を区別しつつ、その先の展開を推論・予測するという読み方は容易にできることではありません。その際に手助けとなるのは「**注釈を付ける**」ことです。注釈は要点を思い出したり、読後に振り返ったりする際に役立ちます。以下は使用する記号の例です。

- 英文の主題（文、語句）⇒ **下線**
- 事実を含む箇所 ⇒ 欄外に **F**　(= fact)
- 著者の意見（賛成）⇒ 欄外に **A**　(= agree)
- 著者の意見（同意できない）⇒ 欄外に **D**　(= disagree)
- 結論 ⇒ **二重線**
- 興味深い内容 ⇒ 欄外に○
- 理解できない箇所 ⇒ 欄外に？

この章の英文では第 1 パラグラフの living in a van ... amenities と vanliving に下線、最終パラグラフの 1 行目にある結論 We may conclude that ... "vanlife" の箇所に二重線を引きます。さらに、同パラグラフ内で著者の意見を表す I believe ..., In my opinion ..., It seems to me that ... についてそれぞれ賛成できれば「A」、そうでなければ「D」を欄外に記入します。この英文では事実が多く提示されるので「F」は重要と思う箇所のみ欄外に記入するとよいでしょう。

B　Discussion

Discuss the following statements or questions.

1. Based on the information provided in the reading passage, discuss the advantages and disadvantages of "vanlife."

2. If you could, would you choose to live a "vanlife"? Why or why not?

Chapter 11   Van Living

A Build Your Vocabulary

Find the words in the reading passage that match the definitions below.

1. (line 7) a person who lives in a particular place = _____

2. (line 12) to follow or try to catch something = _____

3. (line 19) larger than necessary = _____

4. (line 23) a thing that is absolutely necessary = _____

5. (line 25) to do something that is required = _____

6. (line 27) coming after = _____

7. (line 43) a problem or disadvantage = _____

8. (line 44) based on sound reason = _____

B Summary & Dictation

 70

Complete the paragraph with the words below. Change the word form if necessary. Listen to the passage to check the answers.

- remote   - income   - equip   - scarce   - recession
- necessity   - nomad   - embrace   - widespread   - fund

The U.S. movie *Nomadland* depicted older Americans who lead a ①[   ] van-based lifestyle, not by choice but out of ②[   ]. An increasing number of senior citizens are finding it impossible to retire because they receive little or no ③[   ] from a pension and have no savings. Many therefore ④[   ] a van with some basic essentials and drive around the country in search of work. In the financial crash of 2008 and the subsequent ⑤[   ], many Americans lost their houses, jobs, and retirement ⑥[   ]. If they were living in an area where jobs were ⑦[   ] or where accommodation costs were high, living in a van offered a solution. Many younger people also ⑧[   ] it as a lifestyle choice. With ⑨[   ] working becoming more established as a result of the COVID-19 pandemic and the ⑩[   ] availability of high-speed Internet service, it is now possible to work while on the road.

74

Chapter 12

Sportswashing

2022年のワールドカップサッカートーナメントが開催されたカタールには、それ以前にサッカースタジアムもプロチームもなく、何より気候的にサッカーに適さない国でした。どのような経緯でこの地で世界大会が開催されるに至ったのでしょう。

Before You Read

Complete the sentences below.

1. The decision to award Qatar hosting rights for the 2022 Soccer World Cup was [understandable / surprising] for many people.
2. The schedule for the matches at the Qatar World Cup [fitted in with / disrupted] the normal soccer schedule in most competing countries.
3. "Sportswashing" is a term that refers to a type of [honest / dishonest] behavior.
4. The 2022 Qatar World Cup was generally considered to have been a [success / failure] in several ways.
5. In order to build stadiums and infrastructure for the event, Qatar employed thousands of [domestic / foreign] workers.

Let Sports Clean Up Your Image

1 There is no doubt that people everywhere get joy and excitement from watching the world's best athletes come together to compete at the very highest level. But more and more people are beginning to be disturbed by the way sports are becoming **entangled with** big money and politics.

2 As an example of this, many people saw Qatar's hosting of the soccer World Cup in 2022 as an example of so-called "sportswashing." "Sportswashing," which may be an unfamiliar word, describes a practice **whereby** countries or organizations with a poor human rights record use a major sporting event as a way to improve their global image. For example, Qatar, a tiny desert kingdom in the Middle East, has often been criticized for its restrictions on freedom of expression, harassment of human rights activists and journalists, and discrimination against women and LGBTQ+ people.

3 This raised a question in the minds of many people: **in the face of** so many negative factors, why did FIFA (the governing body of world soccer) decide to award the hosting of the competition to Qatar? FIFA said it was a way to expand the reach of soccer to the Middle East, where the sport is relatively undeveloped.

4 A more interesting question, though, may be why Qatar was so eager to host the tournament considering the massive financial and **infrastructural** hurdles that the country would face. Qatar, with a population of just 2.7 million people, had no soccer tradition and no professional

Vocabulary

entangled with ~
～と関わって

whereby ~
それにより～する

in the face of ~
～に直面して

infrastructural
経済基盤の

soccer teams. What is more, the country did not have enough stadiums of the required standard, meaning that it would have to **embark on** a massive program of construction and **renovation**.

5   Another problem was Qatar's climate. Average summer temperatures can exceed 45ºC, and so the tournament was moved to November and December, a move that **disrupted** the normal soccer schedule in many of the competing countries. A further **complicating** factor was the fact that more than one million visitors were expected to attend, which required building more than 100 new hotels. In the end, it was estimated that Qatar spent more than $200 billion on staging the competition, making it the most expensive World Cup ever held.

6   In the end, the final results of the 2022 World Cup were mixed. Fortunately for Qatar and FIFA, the competition **ended up** go**ing** smoothly. It was generally considered a success, with high-quality soccer, exciting matches, and record-breaking TV audiences around the world. However, whether it succeeded in improving Qatar's global image is a different matter. In order to complete the enormous construction projects on schedule, Qatar had to import thousands of workers from countries such as India, Pakistan, Nepal, and Bangladesh. These workers **reportedly** had to tolerate extremely harsh working and living conditions. Although Qatar authorities dispute the numbers, it is estimated that more than 6,500 of these workers died in the **runup to** the competition.

---

embark on ~
〜に着手する
renovation 改築

disrupt ~
〜を中断させる
complicating
複雑な、厄介な

end up ~ing
最終的に〜する

reportedly
伝えられたところによる
と

runup to ~
〜までの 準備期間

Chapter 12　Sportswashing

77

A Overview

Read the passage and choose the correct statement from each pair.

1. a) When Qatar was awarded hosting rights for the 2022 World Cup, it was already engaged in building the necessary infrastructure.
   b) When Qatar was awarded hosting rights for the 2022 World Cup, it lacked both a soccer tradition and sufficient infrastructure.
2. a) There are suspicions that financial irregularities played a part in Qatar being chosen as host country.
   b) The strong soccer culture in the Middle East was the main reason behind Qatar being chosen as host country.
3. a) "Sportswashing" refers to an attempt to use sport to shift attention away from a country's negative aspects.
   b) "Sportswashing" refers to organizing a major international sports event in a country where it has never been held before.
4. a) A number of matches in the Qatar World Cup had to be rescheduled because of temperatures exceeding 45 degrees Celsius.
   b) The Qatar World Cup was held toward the end of the year to avoid problems caused by the country's excessive summer heat.
5. a) The 2022 Qatar World Cup greatly improved the country's overall image on the international stage.
   b) The 2022 Qatar World Cup may not have achieved all the results the country was hoping for.

B Focus on Details

Read the passage again and complete each sentence.

1. Qatar had no soccer tradition and no professional soccer teams. _____ is more, the country did not have enough stadiums.
   a) Which   b) What   c) This   d) That
2. A further _____ factor was the fact that more than one million visitors were expected to attend.
   a) complicate   b) complication   c) complicated   d) complicating
3. A more interesting question may be why Qatar wanted to host the tournament _____ the massive financial and infrastructural hurdles.
   a) despite   b) besides   c) although   d) even
4. Qatar had long faced criticism in several areas, including discrimination _____ women and LGBTQ + people.
   a) among   b) with   c) against   d) for
5. The 2022 World Cup was generally considered a success. _____ it succeeded in improving Qatar's global image is a different matter.
   a) While   b) Whether   c) When   d) Whereas

78

Chapter 12　Sportswashing

A　Zoom In

ポスト・リーディング とは

ポスト・リーディング（post-reading）とは英文内容を理解した後で行う「**振り返り**」を言いますが、クリティカル・リーディングにおいては「プレ」や「ホワイル」と同等、場合によってそれ以上に重要なステップになり得ます。

1. 情報を抽出する
   自分で記入した注釈を元に英文から情報を抜き出す
2. 概要をまとめる（＋要約する）
   抜き出した情報を元に概要を作成する（＋概要を元に要約文を書く）
3. 反応する
   英文内容に関する感想を表現する

批判的読解のポイントは英文を通して与えられた情報を自主的に整理し、それを元に内容に対して反応することです。すでにこの章の英文 Sportswashing を読み終えているのであればカタールで開催された華やかな World Cup in 2022 の裏側について何かしらの感情を抱いたと思います。以降の Zoom In では、それらのまとめ方について解説します。

B　Discussion

Discuss the following statements or questions.

1. Are you for or against Qatar having organized the 2022 World Cup in order to improve their global reputation?

2. Name any worldwide sport event ever held in Japan (e.g., the 2020 Tokyo Olympics). Did it contribute to raising the global image of Japan? How?

Wrap-up

A Build Your Vocabulary

Find the words in the reading passage that match the definitions below.

1. (line 4) to make somebody worry = _____
2. (line 13) a law or rule that limits something = _____
3. (line 22) to a fairly high degree = _____
4. (line 25) very large in size = _____
5. (line 25) a problem or difficulty to be dealt with = _____
6. (line 40) to present to an audience = _____
7. (line 52) to put up with = _____
8. (line 53) to question whether something is true = _____

B Summary & Dictation

Complete the paragraph with the words below. Change the word form if necessary. Listen to the passage to check the answers.

| • expand | • factor | • allege | • bid | • discriminate |
| • massive | • restrict | • develop | • critic | • harass |

In the face of many negative ①[   ], including lack of a soccer tradition, inadequate infrastructure, and an unsuitable climate, FIFA decided to award the 2022 Soccer World Cup to Qatar. FIFA said it was a way to ②[   ] the reach of soccer to the Middle East, where the sport is relatively ③[   ]. However, there have been several ④[   ] of bribery and corruption in the ⑤[   ] process. A more interesting question may be why Qatar wanted to host the tournament despite ⑥[   ] financial and infrastructural hurdles. Many people have seen Qatar's hosting of the World Cup as "sportswashing," a term that describes countries or organizations with a poor human rights record using a major sporting event as a way to improve their global image. Qatar had long faced ⑦[   ] in several areas, including ⑧[   ] on freedom of expression, ⑨[   ] of human rights activists and journalists, and ⑩[   ] against women and LGBTQ+ people.

Chapter 13
Board Games and Climate Change

大多数の人は環境問題に取り組む必要性を意識しつつ、実際に何から始めるべきか思いつきません。そのような場合にはボードゲームが大いに役立ちます。ボードゲームはどのような利点があり、どのようなボードゲームが有益なのでしょう。

 Before You Read

Complete the sentences below.

1. In the past few years, the United States has been [hit by / free from] catastrophic weather events.
2. Several recent board games [ignore / address] environmental issues.
3. Being forced to stay at home during the COVID-19 pandemic has [boosted / dampened] people's interest in board games.
4. Unlike large manufacturers, some small game designers now specifically target [children / adults].
5. One good thing about board games is that they often [foster / discourage] personal interaction.

Everyone Is a Winner

1   Recently, we have experienced a growing number of **catastrophic** weather events: record heatwaves in Europe, wildfires in Australia and California, along with droughts and intense hurricanes in the United States. It is now impossible to deny that Earth's climate is undergoing profound and worrying changes.

2   If we care for our beautiful planet, it is up to us to tackle climate change, but the scale and **complexity** of the problem make it difficult to know where to start. I would suggest that one extremely effective way to start raising awareness is through board games, however unlikely that may sound. In recent years, some of the most popular games on the market have been ones dealing with environmental issues.

3   These days, board games are no longer a niche interest, popular only among a small group of enthusiasts. On the contrary, their popularity is **snowballing**. Partly, this is due to people being forced to stay at home by the COVID-19 pandemic. According to a report by a research organization, the global market for such games is growing rapidly and is predicted to be worth $12 billion by 2026. In 2019, the fastest-growing types of cafés and bars in the world were those devoted to board games. And in 2020, sales of board games on Amazon rose by 40 percent.

4   In addition to giant brands like Hasbro and Mattel, which focus on children's games, the market has grown to **encompass** small designers who **specialize in** making

Vocabulary

catastrophic 壊滅的な

complexity 複雑さ

snowball
(雪だるま式に) 高まる

encompass ~
~を取り巻く
specialize in ~
~を専門とする

games that target adults. Several recent offerings are environmentally themed. The following are some of my favorites. In the award-winning game Wingspan, which sold over 750,000 copies in its first year, players develop **biodiverse** bird habitats, while players in the game Kyoto take on the roles of negotiators at an international climate conference. Players in Tipping Point must build cities that adapt to climate change.

5 There is another feature of board games that I particularly appreciate. In contrast to the physical isolation of online gaming, board games foster personal interaction by requiring players to collaborate with others. Environmentally themed games **capitalize on** this. Whereas conventional board games focus on one player achieving total victory in **zero-sum** competitions, this new genre of games emphasizes cooperation, which I believe becomes the key to success. For me, this naturally reflects how we must act in the real world if we are to succeed in solving climate-based problems.

6 It is my firm belief that playing climate-centered board games can be effective in raising awareness, especially among the younger generation. I am convinced that by presenting the reality of climate change **in a concentrated** and simplified **way**, such games help players gain a deeper understanding of the issues involved and increase their sense of environmental responsibility.

biodiverse 多種多様な

capitalize on ~
〜に乗じる

zero-sum
全員の得点の総和がゼロ
になる

in a concentrated way
集約的に

A Overview

Read the passage and choose the correct statement from each pair.

1. a) In recent years, the U.S. has experienced both lack of rainfall and powerful storms.
   b) In recent years, Europe has experienced record heatwaves and wildfires.
2. a) Online gaming has boomed since the beginning of the COVID-19 pandemic.
   b) One effect of the COVID-19 pandemic has been a boost in the popularity of board games.
3. a) Playing board games is mostly restricted to people playing in their own homes.
   b) There is a growing number of commercial venues that target customers who want to play board games.
4. a) Adults have become the target customers for some smaller board game designers.
   b) Large board game manufacturers such as Hasbro and Mattel are now increasingly targeting adult players.
5. a) Environmentally themed games tend to prioritize collaboration over competition.
   b) Online games are designed to foster personal interaction among players.

B Focus on Details

Read the passage again and complete each sentence.

1. Recently, there have been more and more _____ weather events around the world.
   a) catastrophe   b) catastrophized   c) catastrophizing   d) catastrophic
2. Current board games are far _____ being an interest for just tiny groups of enthusiasts.
   a) away   b) from   c) with   d) out
3. The aim of the game *Tipping Point* is to have players build cities that _____ to climate change.
   a) adapt   b) adopt   c) adjoin   d) address
4. _____ conventional board games focus on one player winning total victory, these new games emphasize cooperation.
   a) Because   b) Whereas   c) Although   d) Before
5. There is evidence that climate-themed board games are _____ in raising people's awareness of environmental issues.
   a) affective   b) affordable   c) efficient   d) effective

Chapter 13　Board Games and Climate Change

Follow-up

A Zoom In

ポスト・リーディング 1：情報を抽出する

往々にして英文を通して得た情報や想起された感情は英文を読み終えた段階で忘れてしまいますが、読み終えた英文から「**情報を抽出する**」ことで記憶を辿って新たな視点で内容を整理することができます。その際には読解中に付けた注釈（Unit 11 参照）を活用して、以下の①〜③の情報を特定します。

> ①主題 ⇐ **下線**を引いた箇所
> ②主題を支持する事実 ⇐ 欄外に記入した **F**
> ③結論 ⇐ **二重線**を引いた箇所

この章の英文は事実に基づくものなので、第1パラグラフを始め②に関する情報を見つけるのは比較的容易です。しかしながら、①主題は第2パラグラフの I would suggest that . . .（私は〜を提案したい）、③結論は最後のパラグラフの I am totally convinced that . . .（私は〜と完全に確信している）に書かれているので、注釈を付けておかないと読後に見つけるのは手間がかかります。これら3つの情報を抜き出すことで簡略的なパラグラフ構造が提示されます。

B Discussion

Discuss the following statements or questions.

1. Have you ever played a game (e.g., board game, video game, mobile game) that is practically or educationally useful? What did you learn?

2. Other than playing games, what are fun and effective ways in raising awareness about environmental issues?

Wrap-up

A Build Your Vocabulary

Find the words in the reading passage that match the definitions below.

1. (line 6) strongly influential = _____
2. (line 8) to try to deal with something difficult = _____
3. (line 11) understanding that something is happening = _____
4. (line 15) appealing to a particular section of the population = _____
5. (line 23) having strong love for something = _____
6. (line 28) a thing produced for entertainment = _____
7. (line 38) to encourage or promote something = _____
8. (line 49) having a strong belief = _____

B Summary & Dictation

 84

Complete the paragraph with the words below. Change the word form if necessary. Listen to the passage to check the answers.

| • snowball | • aware | • emphasize | • encompass | • enthusiast |
| • zero-sum | • biodiverse | • rapid | • negotiate | • evidence |

These days, board games are far from being popular only among a small group of ①[   ]. On the contrary, their popularity is ②[   ]. According to a report by the research organization Research and Markets, the global market for such games is growing ③[   ]. In 2019, the fastest-growing types of cafés and bars in the world were devoted to board games. The board game market now ④[   ] small designers who specialize in games that target adults. Several recent offerings are environmentally themed. In the award-winning game *Wingspan*, players develop ⑤[   ] bird habitats, while players in the game *Kyoto* play the roles of ⑥[   ] at an international climate conference. Whereas conventional board games focus on one player achieving total victory in ⑦[   ] competitions, this new genre of games ⑧[   ] cooperation, which becomes the key to success. ⑨[   ] suggests that playing climate-centered board games can be effective in raising environmental ⑩[   ].

Chapter 14: The Gig Economy

フードデリバリーや動画編集を始め、多種多様な業種において「ギグ」という働き方が一般的になりつつあります。「ギグワーク」の長所と短所、適している人や不向きな人などについて改めて考えてみましょう。

Complete the sentences below.

1. The word "gig," which is often used by musicians or other performers, refers to a [single / long-term] engagement.
2. The word "gig" is now [seldom / commonly] used outside the world of music and performing.
3. Around [10 percent / one third] of U.S. workers are now active in the gig economy.
4. People who do gig work appreciate the [stability / flexibility] that this kind of work offers.
5. Working in the gig economy is more likely to suit those [with / without] family responsibilities.

Reading Passage

Freedom or Security ?

1　As an amateur musician in my younger days, I would always **pester** my friends with questions like, "Do you want to come to my **gig** on Saturday?" In the music world, "gig" means a one-time performance. However, I gave up my ambition to become a professional musician when I realized that most musicians have little or no prospect of steady full-time employment, so their ability to earn a living through music depends on finding a succession of **one-off** engagements, or gigs.

2　Increasingly, the word "gig" is no longer confined to the world of music as the so-called "gig economy" becomes a more widespread feature of labor markets around the world. The gig economy is characterized by flexible, temporary, or freelance jobs that often involve connecting with clients through online platforms. Some typical examples of gig economy work include driving for **ride-hailing** services (e.g. Uber), delivering food (e.g. Uber Eats), or providing services such as graphic design or computer code writing. It is estimated that, as of 2021, around one third of the labor force in the U.S. was involved in this style of work.

3　Gig work can undoubtedly benefit both employers and workers. It gives companies greater flexibility in hiring. Some firms cannot afford to hire full-time workers, and so will **take on** gig workers to help out at particularly busy times. Even some richer companies use the same strategy as it enables them to cut costs and make greater savings on their payroll. Also, advances in IT mean that many different

Vocabulary

pester A with B
AをBでしつこく悩みます

gig
(単発の)ライブ、演奏会

one-off　1回限りの

ride-hailing　配車

take on ~　~を雇用する

kinds of work can be done **remotely**, and so employers
now have access to a vastly expanded **pool of labor**, eliminating the need to rely on people living close to the workplace. Similarly, flexibility is also a great attraction for workers in the gig economy. They can choose when, where, and for whom to work and can often set their own schedules.

4   Despite these apparent attractions, the gig economy has significant **downsides**. In my view, the most serious is a lack of traditional employment benefits. As a gig worker, you are not an employee in the usual sense; rather, you are **classified as** an independent contractor or self-employed. **Aside from** being paid a fee for your work, you will receive none of the benefits of being an official employee, such as health insurance, paid leave, or retirement plans. Additionally, you are responsible for your own taxes and expenses.

5   The gig economy may suit people who are younger, single, and prepared to tolerate a degree of financial uncertainty in exchange for working on their own terms. But for older people, especially those who have family responsibilities, this style of work can cause **considerable** stress. And unfortunately, as more and more companies recognize the **upside** of contracting workers on this basis, the number of steady full-time positions available is likely to **dwindle**.

---

remotely
インターネット経由で、リモートで
pool of labor 労働要員

downside マイナス面

classify ～ as . . .
～を…に分類する
aside from ～
～の他には

considerable 相当な

upside プラス面

dwindle 減少する

A Overview

Read the passage and choose the correct statement from each pair.

1. a) The gig economy is becoming a common feature of labor markets around the world.
   b) At present, the only country where the gig economy is a feature of the labor market is the U.S.
2. a) Jobs in the gig economy are confined mostly to ride-hailing and food delivery services.
   b) The range of jobs available in the gig economy is getting wider all the time.
3. a) Some firms need workers at only certain times of the year, so employing gig workers is a good strategy.
   b) Most companies prefer to employ full-time staff who are constantly available to work.
4. a) Some people like to be self-employed because it is one legitimate way to avoid paying tax.
   b) Self-employed workers are not eligible for benefits such as health insurance and paid vacation.
5. a) Some gig workers may believe that working on their own terms is preferable to guaranteed financial stability.
   b) It is probably more common to find older people rather than younger people working in the gig economy.

B Focus on Details

Read the passage again and complete each sentence.

1. Musicians' ability to earn a living through music is _____ upon finding a succession of one-off gigs.
   a) depend   b) depended   c) dependent   d) depends
2. Some firms cannot afford to hire full-time workers, and so will take _____ gig workers to help out at particularly busy times.
   a) on   b) in   c) out   d) over
3. _____ from being paid a fee for their work, they receive none of the benefits associated with being an official employee.
   a) Except   b) Rather   c) Aside   d) Unlike
4. _____ more companies recognize the upside of hiring gig workers, the number of full-time positions available is likely to dwindle.
   a) Before   b) As   c) Although   d) Until
5. Unfortunately, most musicians have little or no _____ of securing steady full-time employment.
   a) prospect   b) program   c) preview   d) preparation

Chapter 14　The Gig Economy

ポスト・リーディング2：概要をまとめる

注釈を付けて抜きだした情報を体系的に整理する（→ Unit 13）と英文の「**概要をまとめる**」（要約する）ことができます。本章の英文においては、抜き出した情報を「主題」「事実」「結論」に選別すると以下のようになります。

主題
"Gig economy" becomes a more widespread feature of labor markets around the world.

事実
・プラス面
Gig work can undoubtedly benefit both employers and workers.
・マイナス面
The gig economy has significant downsides, the most serious of which is lack of traditional employment benefits.

結論
As more and more companies recognize the upside of contracting workers on this basis, the number of steady full-time positions available is likely to dwindle.

さらにこれらの文を接続詞（but など）や接続副詞（therefore など）を用いて整えることで短い要約文を作成できます。概要をまとめ、要約する際には、各段落の役割を踏まえてそれぞれの段落の中で最も重要な文を見つけるようにしましょう。

B Discussion

Discuss the following statements or questions.

1. Based on the reading passage, discuss the advantages and disadvantages of doing gig work.

2. If you desperately need to earn some money in a short period of time, which type of work would you choose, working part-time or doing gig work? Why?

Chapter 14　The Gig Economy

Wrap-up

A Build Your Vocabulary

Find the words in the reading passage that match the definitions below.

1. (line 6) the possibility that something good will happen　= _____
2. (line 8) a following of one thing after another　= _____
3. (line 10) to limit an activity in some way　= _____
4. (line 13) to describe the special qualities of something　= _____
5. (line 37) important enough to be noticed　= _____
6. (line 40) working for oneself, not for an employer　= _____
7. (line 46) to be satisfactory to someone　= _____
8. (line 48) a condition of an agreement　= _____

B Summary & Dictation

Complete the paragraph with the words below. Change the word form if necessary. Listen to the passage to check the answers.

| •flexible | •typical | •expand | •character | •remote |
| •advance | •attract | •similar | •benefit | •afford |

The gig economy is ①[　　　　　　] by flexible, temporary, or freelance jobs that often involve connecting with clients through some kind of online platform. The range of such jobs is constantly ②[　　　　　　], but some ③[　　　　　　] examples of gig economy work include driving for ride-hailing services or delivering food. Gig work can ④[　　　　　　] both employers and workers. It gives companies much greater ⑤[　　　　　　] in hiring. Some firms cannot ⑥[　　　　　　] to hire full-time workers, and so will take on gig workers to help out at busy times. Even some richer companies use the same strategy because it allows them to cut costs. ⑦[　　　　　　] in IT mean that many kinds of work can be done ⑧[　　　　　　], and so employers now have access to an expanded pool of labor. ⑨[　　　　　　], flexibility is also a great ⑩[　　　　　　] for workers in the gig economy. They can choose when, where, and for whom to work and can often set their own schedules.

Chapter 15
Digital Music

デジタル技術の進化により、ダウンロードやストリーミングを通して誰もが手軽に音楽を聞ける時代になりました。音楽制作も飛躍的変化を遂げましたが、簡単に作曲、配信できることには従来とは異なる苦労が伴います。デジタル音楽の功罪とは何でしょう。

Before You Read

Complete the sentences below.

1. The golden era of pop music began in the [1960s / 1970s].
2. Nowadays, the barriers to producing and distributing music are [higher / lower] than they have ever been.
3. Digital technology has made the process of recording music much [easier to control / more difficult to manage].
4. Current methods of music distribution [require / have eliminated] much physical labor.
5. Digital technology has made the process of creating music more [democratic / elitist].

Are Computers Destroying Music ?

Vocabulary

1   The golden era of pop music began in the early 1960s with the Beatles in the UK. The Beatles were truly exceptional in terms of talent, creativity, and musicianship, **not to mention** their phenomenal global success. Yet, in other ways, their story was typical for bands of their time. They **honed** their skills by performing countless shows in small clubs. They acquired a manager who had confidence in their ability and was able to negotiate a contract with a record company, which provided an **advance payment** to cover the considerable costs of recording. The company also paid for manufacturing the band's records and shipping them to stores around the UK and other countries. For the Beatles and bands like them, the journey from unknown band to successful pop stars was long, complex, and costly.

not to mention ~
〜は言うまでもなく

hone ~
〜に磨きをかける

advance payment
前払い金

2   Today, the process of both producing and distributing music has changed radically, principally because of digital technology. First, let's look at the process of recording. Until digital recording technology became established, musicians would record directly onto giant tape machines. Often, they would play together live in the studio. If a player made a mistake, the recording would have to **start** again **from scratch**. With digital technology, however, each voice and instrument can be recorded separately on an individual track. The recording engineer can fix mistakes in tempo or pitch with just a few mouse clicks. What is more, the sound of **virtually any** instrument can be digitally generated if necessary.

start ~ from scratch
〜をゼロから始める

virtually any ~
事実上いかなる〜

3   Next, let's look at distribution. Traditionally, music

was distributed **physically** in the form of vinyl records,
30 cassette tapes, or CDs. Manufacturing and shipping these items required money and labor. With the **advent** of music streaming and download services such as Spotify and Apple Music, the need for physical distribution of music has **dwindled** considerably. Most music fans now
35 consume music in digital form through online services, and hardly ever buy a physical product.

4 **In a sense**, digital technology has "democratized" the process of creating music. With basic knowledge of inexpensive recording software, musicians can now
40 produce professional-level recordings on a laptop computer at home. **When it comes to** distribution, they can reach the public through social media platforms such as YouTube, Instagram, and TikTok.

5 **All in all**, can we say that the development of
45 digital music has been a good thing? Personally, I consider it a disaster for music as a whole. It has led millions of people to believe that music is a free resource, just like the air that we breathe. Music streaming companies such as Apple, Spotify, and YouTube have **taken advantage of**
50 this to pay musicians tiny amounts for their music, making it increasingly difficult for them to make a living from their art.

---

physically
物(体)として

advent 到来

dwindle
徐々に減少する

in a sense ある意味

when it comes to ~
～に関して言えば

all in all 全体的に見て

taken advantage of ~
～に便乗する

 **Test Yourself**

A Overview

Read the passage and choose the correct statement from each pair.

1. a) Despite their talent, the Beatles' path to success was the same as for other bands of the era.
   b) By sheer luck, the Beatles were able to discover a new and quicker way to become pop stars.
2. a) The sound of most instruments that we hear in songs these days has been digitally generated.
   b) Digital technology gives recording engineers a high level of control over recorded tracks.
3. a) If home recording software were not so expensive, more people would be recording music at home.
   b) Recording professional-sounding music at relatively low cost is now within the reach of more and more people.
4. a) Music distribution no longer relies predominantly on producing, transporting, and selling physical items.
   b) Music fans nowadays tend to purchase physical items because they are much less expensive than before.
5. a) Nowadays, most people are happy to pay high prices to buy the music they like.
   b) Nowadays, many people believe that music is basically free.

B Focus on Details

Read the passage again and complete each sentence.

1. The Beatles were truly exceptional in _____ of their talent, creativity, and musicianship.
   a) regard   b) connection   c) terms   d) relation
2. Today, the process of both producing and distributing music has _____ radical changes.
   a) understood   b) underestimated   c) underlined   d) undergone
3. _____ digital recording technology became established, musicians would record directly onto giant tape machines.
   a) Until   b) Since   c) After   d) While
4. What is more, the sound of virtually any instrument can be digitally generated if _____.
   a) need   b) needing   c) necessity   d) necessary
5. When it _____ to distribution, they can reach the public through social media platforms
   a) goes   b) comes   c) concerns   d) involves

Chapter 15　Digital Music

A Zoom In

ポスト・リーディング3：反応する

英文を正確かつ深く理解すると、内容に関して「なるほど興味深い」「自分はそう思わない」といった「**反応をする**」のは自然なことです。英文を読み終えた後、記入した注釈（→ Unit 11）を見返しながら、以下の質問を自問自答してみましょう。

> ①自分の興味・関心（どの箇所が面白いと思ったか）　⇐　欄外の ✓
> ②提示された事実（情報は未知のものか、不足しているか）　⇐　欄外の **F**
> ③著者の意見（著者の意見についてどう思うか）　⇐　欄外の **A** または **D**

本章の英文であれば、①については主題（デジタル音楽）の性質から✓の数が多いと思われますが、トピックに詳しい方であれば②については「情報が足りない」と感じるかも知れません。さらに最後のパラグラフで著者はデジタル音楽の発展について Personally, I consider it a disaster for music as a whole. と述べていますが、「そう思わない」（③は「D」）という人もいるでしょう。クリティカル・リーディングで最も重要なのは英語を通して仕入れた情報に対して自身の感情を呼び起こし、明示的に反応することです。

B Discussion

Discuss the following statements or questions.

1. Have you ever bought physical musical products such as CDs and DVDs? If yes, what made you do it? If not, why didn't you do it?

2. If you were a musician composing music, what would you do to make your own works clearly distinct from other musicians'?

Chapter 15 Digital Music

Wrap-up

A Build Your Vocabulary

Find the words in the reading passage that match the definitions below.

1. (line 2) much greater than usual = _____
2. (line 4) extremely successful = _____
3. (line 6) very many = _____
4. (line 10) rather large in amount = _____
5. (line 16) to spread the product throughout the marketplace = _____
6. (line 16) completely = _____
7. (line 35) to use something = _____
8. (line 46) a complete failure = _____

B Summary & Dictation

 96

Complete the paragraph with the words below. Change the word form if necessary. Listen to the passage to check the answers.

| • establish | • individual | • radical | • dwindle | • virtual |
| • traditional | • generate | • manufacture | • separate | • consume |

Today, the process of producing and distributing music has undergone ①[   ] changes because of digital technology. Until digital recording technology became ②[   ], musicians would record directly onto giant tape machines. Often, they would play together live in the studio. If a player made a mistake, the recording would have to start again. With digital technology, however, each voice and instrument can be recorded ③[   ] on an ④[   ] track. The recording engineer can fix mistakes in tempo or pitch with just a few clicks of a mouse. What is more, the sound of ⑤[   ] any instrument can be digitally ⑥[   ] if necessary. ⑦[   ], music was distributed physically in the form of vinyl records, cassette tapes, or CDs. ⑧[   ] and shipping these items required money and labor. With the advent of music streaming and download services, the need for physical distribution of music has ⑨[   ] considerably. Most music fans now ⑩[   ] music in digital form through online services.

TEXT PRODUCTION STAFF

edited by	編集
Hiroko Nakazawa	中澤 ひろ子

English-language editing by	英文校閲
Bill Benfield	ビル・ベンフィールド

cover design by	表紙デザイン
Nobuyoshi Fujino	藤野 伸芳

CD PRODUCTION STAFF

recorded by	吹き込み者
Howard Colefield (AmE)	ハワード・コルフィールド（アメリカ英語）
Jennifer Okano (AmE)	ジェニファー・オカノ（アメリカ英語）

Reading Palette Blue —Intermediate—
英文読解への多面的アプローチ〈中級〉
クリティカル・リーディング

2025年1月20日　初版発行
2025年2月15日　第2刷発行

著　　者　武藤 克彦・Bill Benfield

発 行 者　佐野 英一郎

発 行 所　株式会社 成 美 堂
　　　　　〒101-0052　東京都千代田区神田小川町3-22
　　　　　TEL 03-3291-2261　FAX 03-3293-5490
　　　　　https://www.seibido.co.jp

印 刷・製 本　三美印刷株式会社

ISBN 978-4-7919-7305-7　　　　　　　　　　　　　Printed in Japan

・落丁・乱丁本はお取り替えします。
・本書の無断複写は、著作権上の例外を除き著作権侵害となります。